BALANCING

DARK WITH

LIGHT

A Journey from Ghetto to God

Anthony D. Vaughn

Table of Contents

Hello World!

Sunday, August 4, 1985, at 1:55 pm in Waukegan, Illinois, the time, date, and place in which a handsome little boy by the name of Anthony Ditrail Vaughn was born. This baby may have seemed like any other baby, with his mom's mucus and feces all around him, but he wasn't like any other baby. Why? The reason this baby was different because he had his own particular set of trials, tribulations, and victories to encounter. Hello World!

This young man was born to a beautiful, talented, and sensitive young mother by the name of Regina Vaughn. She was just 16yrs and 4 days old when she gave birth to me. She was a young woman with so much promise because of her natural gifts and abilities, but tragedy struck at the tender young age of 14. Her mother died of complications from high blood pressure due in part to an addiction to food.

She had 3 older sisters Linda, Renee' and Theresa all of who had moved out leaving her, her older brother Louis Jr., and her dad Louis Sr. Her dad had been going to school at UCLA to become a doctor, until he gave it all up to pursue a more important subject to study, my grandmother, the beautiful, brick-house by the name of Dorthy Bell Elizabeth Jane Denton. Now he was a machinist laboring and providing for his family at the US Steel Corporation in Gary, Indiana. After losing the love of his life, Grandad, sad with grief and memories of Grandma began doing his best to get over the pain. He did that by turning to alcohol, eventually becoming consumed by the heartache and pain that he felt only the bottle could take away. This was even more challenging to my young mother who now only had her brother, Louis to lean on.

Louis was just like any other high school teens at that time in the 70s. He was mischievous and exploring all the fun that life had to offer to be in an unstable or any home, marijuana, alcohol, and of course, the "honeys". Although he had his own life he did what he could to take care of his baby sister, but he was graduating high school and had to make a decision. The decision he made was to go to the United States Navy. This was great for him but it was another devastating blow for mom.

My mom met my dad when she was 15 years old and he was 20, back home from college, probably celebrating his birthday since I was conceived around his birthday month. Shortly after I was conceived my grandfather and mother moved back to mom's hometown, Waukegan, Illinois where I was born. My mom and dad both told me that my dad

didn't know that she was pregnant with me. It's my theory that my grandfather decided to move back to their hometown to be around family he could trust because my aunts were also dealing with the loss of my grandmother, pushing them to substance abuse. Their substance of choice was the new, "cool" drug of the late 80s, crack cocaine.

I was then born in the loving atmosphere of my grandmother's side of the family. I'm pretty sure that they showed me all kinds of love, is that I was so cute and irresistible and because every time I visit nowadays it's always a lot of fun. After two years there, my mom and I moved to Michigan with my aunt Theresa and her son, my cousin Marcus Vaughn.

While there for a year, got pregnant with my sister Candis, and my aunt decided to move away and get away from her surroundings, which included her boyfriend at the time, and the drugs that she was using so that she could start a better life outside of her comfort zone, in San Diego, California. At this time after mom had gone through more heartache and pain than many adults by the age of 18, and now she was headed back to live with her alcoholic dad in Gary, Indiana where all of her turmoil had begun.

I want to share a very interesting story here. This story was told to me and Marcus many, many times by Aunt Theresa. He may not care for it so much, but I love it and it'll provide you, the reader an idea of what this book is all about.

4 | BALANCING DARK WITH LIGHT

While in Michigan, Marcus and I were playing with his toys (so cute) both minding our own business, having the time of our baby lives, but somehow our paths crossed and he decided to snatch the toy that I was playing with, making me cry until I went on and began playing with another toy. He then came over to me again and attempted to take the toy away, but instead, I just handed it to him and went about my way to continue my happy fun time. He decides to come and snatch another one of his toys away again, but this time I picked up another one and smacked him with it. Then I went on and continued to play while he cried, but after he finished crying we ended up having more fun playing together.

Now it's up to you to look at this scenario however you

choose. Enjoy and I'll see you at the end of the book.

Gary's Growing Pains

My mom, baby sister, and I all moved back to Gary when I was three years of age. At three years old, my grandfather's the house was a place of constant action and because I was so young, both scared me and made me very curious. There was always music playing, people talking and laughing loudly, arguments, and all type of grown-up games being played, from dominoes, spades, and of course, there was enough alcohol for everyone.

Not only were the adults having fun and enjoying themselves, but the children were too! There were cousins everywhere, adventures around the neighborhood and to the park fights with the other children and of course, lots and lots of candy. There were also walks around the neighborhood with my mom and sister. My mom was now 18 years old and pretty much doing what she wanted to do met my step-father,

Rhymuless Darnell Lenoir who lived just one block up the street from my granddad.

My mom was beautiful, smart, and a brick-house just like her mother and my step-father liked what he saw.

He was a very handsome, charismatic, fiery individual with long curly hair and exuded confidence so I'm pretty sure my mom also liked what she saw. He was also the neighborhood drug dealer, but the issue was that he got high on his own supply. Little did my mom knows, but her, my baby sisters, and my lives were about to change drastically because we had now moved into this new man's house, which she told me to call dad.

This new move came quick and it didn't sit well with my grandfather at all. These two were so much alike that they hated each other. I witnessed more arguments between the two that a young child should. There was nothing they could do but eventually get along because they both loved my mother dearly.

During the next year, I got acquainted with walking back and forth between both houses with my sister and stopping by the candy man's store in the middle. The candy man was white in the middle of a black neighborhood with a candy store in his basement. I don't know if he ever did anything but it just sounds suspicious. Anyway, he didn't bother us because he knew who our families were. Now back to our regularly scheduled program. Thanks for letting me go off track a little bit.

This was 1989, the same year that my newest sister was born to my step-father. Her name, Kashae', spelled with a "K" because she was born on her grandmother's kitchen floor where she was delivered by Aunt Linda. The reason why she was born on the kitchen floor was because my mom was now doing drugs herself, and she, my stepfather, and my aunt were high as a kite at the time.

The family was growing and my mom and step-father were partying more and more. We had so many visitors that our house felt like a hotel, but with no overnight stay policy. The house stunk and the people that went in the rooms normal or even vibrant came out with a distant look in their eyes and acting very strange. I was too young to know exactly what was happening, but I was so sensitive that my moods would change with theirs.

Now that my grandfather was out of the picture because of he had a stroke and was now living under the care of Aunt Renee' I found myself going back and forth to my step-father's mother's house pretty regularly. We didn't have a car, phone, or much food for that matter so we had to find a way to get some type of nourishment whenever they were able to come to their senses and realize that they had four children to feed. So I would go with my mother to different people's houses in the neighborhood and watch as she asked to use their phone so she could get food for her children. I just thought of them as little adventures at the time.

Maybe 20 minutes to an hour later someone would come by and pick us up and we'd head to Granny house. I later found out that grannie used to pay people or have other family members stop what they were doing to come and get us. We

8 | BALANCING DARK WITH LIGHT

children were just happy to be going to granny's house because that's where the food was and she would give us 50 cents to go and spend on any candy we liked!

Being at grannies brought more than enough action, because there were the children of her late daughter living with her, cousins from my step-dads younger and older sister, and great-grand-children that were around the same age as me and my siblings. At this time grannie was nimble and laid down the law whenever anyone would get out of hand. That didn't stop my cousins from running the streets and making money and my dad from running the streets and spending money. She loved her children and grandchildren none the less including the newest sibling of mine, a baby sister, Moniquk, born in February 1991.

Our family had swelled up to seven at this point including mom and dad, but the money was nonexistent due to the fact that my parents continued with a strong addiction to crack cocaine. I was 5 years old at this time, now old enough in my parents' eyes to shoulder some of the responsibilities around the house like making bottles, grabbing whatever mom needed to the baby and going over to the neighbor's house alone to call granny and see if someone could pick us up. I was growing up, much quicker than I probably would've liked, but who else was going to do it.

The year 1992 rolled around and as if there weren't enough children to feed, clothe, and take to granny's house, my parents' came along and had a set of twin boys, Darnell and Donnell which when born, was sent home Darnell was on a heart machine, and Donnell was deeply bowlegged. (Both are now healthy and strong and doing well.) I was now six

years old in kindergarten and had new responsibilities that now included changing diapers, getting urinated on, and making and heating bottles, sometimes feeding one of the twins.

Meanwhile, at granny's house, I would go to the store for her, a parent or any other grown-up that needed something from the store. Life was also getting more strained not just for granny, but for my family, and me in particular. Although my sister Candis wasn't related to the family by blood, she was still, a very young baby when she came around, me on the other hand was not blood, but was a little older and not to mention my name was being called by granny more than others, even if it was just to go to the store for her.

This didn't sit well with the cousins so in came the name calling and teasing, with them letting me know that my mom and I am not part of their family or more specifically I should stop calling their uncle, dad because he's not my "real" father. They would also make fun of me for always having to go to the store for other people and of course they made fun of me because my parents were on drugs, but they would keep the joke to my mom since the other person was their family members.

Not only did they tease me, but they would blame our family for any dysfunction that happened at grannies house. My step-dads, nickname is Goo-Goo, and for the record, my nickname is Boo-man, but that's neither here nor there, but whenever anything would happen like someone drops a cup and breaks it, they, being the cousins would automatically say "It must be one of Goo-Goo's kids." Now imagine that happening multiple times a day, not just when everyone could

hear, but even during the times where an aunt is personally telling this to granny when others aren't around and then comes back and is informed to us by other family members. Now with all of this drama going on at home and Grannys here come two more children. My sister Takita was born in 1993 and the baby a beautiful baby girl with the most unique cry you ever could hear, Kimberly was born in 1995. We could now officially start our own, gang, debate team, a baseball team with a designated hitter and a reserve, or a start a pick up 5 on 5 basketball game. Any way you look at it we were stacked!

This also meant that home life and life at grannies was getting more and more interesting year after year due to the constant accumulation of children and the fact that my parents' drug life was gaining more and more control as the responsibilities of my parents' continued to mount up how would it affect me now that I had school to consider while dealing with home and family life.

Shining through
Darkness

During my childhood, I moved houses six times and I moved schools just as many times, stopping at one of the schools twice and living at grannies twice. Yep, I learned to get used to riding roller coasters at an early age which is probably why I became an adrenaline junkie later in life. This also showed how toxic and unstable my childhood was, but it had little effect on me during my younger years.

When it came to school during the elementary years, there
was no student in my class that could rival me whether in
academics or sports. In kindergarten I attended Spaulding
The elementary school where, although I went to school half a
day, I still managed to steal the heart of my favorite teacher,
Mrs. Stewart, while winning the perfect attendance and
honor awards during both semesters.

12 | BALANCING DARK WITH LIGHT

My next 5 years of my life I went to Charles R. Drew, Daniel
Hale Williams, David O. Duncan, Daniel Webster, and back
to Spaulding elementary, which is now closed. David O.
Duncan is someone who can't be searched and Spaulding I
believe was a made-up name is irrelevant, but the other 3
are people that anyone reading this book should
know just a little bit about it.

After living with my step-father up until six years of age, my
mom and he then split for a little while where I remember
moving in with my aunt to the Dorrie Miller projects which
were a really tough place to live. All of Gary, Indiana was a tough
place to live,especially in the 1990s.

During the 90s, Gary was consistently in the top ten lists of
most dangerous cities in the United States. This city spent the
a whole decade on the murder capital list, spending most of the
time in the top five and a few times Gary, Indiana sat all alone

at number one.

This city was overflowing with gang activity. The gangs of choice were the Vice Lords who wore red and the Gangster Disciples who wore blue. There were many stories of cousins killing cousins and whole family organizations getting busted and sent to jail like a family and rap organization called CCA who were indicted by a federal grand jury in 2001. The neighborhood that they were arrested in called Concord village, which is another project that my family moved into after they were all taken into custody. CCA stood for Concord Affiliated which was their rap group's name. A rap group that was beginning to receive national recognition at the time. All now serving life in prison.

I had a cousin who was in one of the gangs go to prison for 15 years for gang activity. He's now out working well and doing everything he can to make sure he stays out. He's someone who I respected enough to write later in life to have him write me back and give me words of encouragement. I'm happy to see him doing well and staying positive.

These are the streets that I had to navigate while heading back and forth to school, but I had little to no fear because of it was just home to me. It was normal. As I walked back and forth to school, some days with my mom and other days with my aunt staying with me until I reached the outskirts of the neighborhood, I would go and continue to excel in my school work, again making the honor roll all four marking periods. I was seven years old at the time.

At eight years old I and the whole family moved in with granny and that made everyone happy except for granny, although she never showed it. She had many more mouths to feed including the grandchildren that lived with her, but by this time they were old enough to feed themselves, and they did with their fast-food jobs and their jobs hustling and making money on the streets.

This is a time where I would see cousins run in the house as if nothing happened after being chased by the police and other cousins driving by in a brand new or an old car that he managed to getaway. Yes, the car did belong to someone and he was just borrowing it for a little while. This is also where I learned that it didn't matter if a girl was ugly or not. I shouldn't let that ever get in my way because a woman's genitals don't have a face. This is advice that got deeper and

more profound the older I got. I'm also pretty sure that at the time he wasn't telling me this for philosophical reasons. This is also a time when walking to the corner store to get some snacks my girl cousin saw a man lying on the ground in blood after being shot to death. Then hearing this I and all my cousins ran to go and see the dead body, but only saw the tape that had outlined where he was. This is the same store that some guys around my age tried to rob me for some food stamps after coming out of the store from getting some groceries for granny. They didn't get the stamps, but they did manage to punch me in the back of the head before I ran to go and get my cousins.

Then there was the third grade where we had then moved to the Delany Projects on street named Fillmore. This was a one way in and one way out the street and at this time during my 94-95 school year the name was known all over Gary as "Killmore" street and I was most definitely a witness to this fact leaving out of the house on my way to school one morning. Although I didn't see the person get shot because that happened the night before, I did see the dead the body lying on the ground the next morning. That still didn't stop my school work from getting done and it surely didn't stop me from winning or coming in the top three in my class in the athletic races.

From there we moved to an area called Glen Park. This is where I spent my time in the fourth grade where I finally had a couple of friends that I could play with across the street and along with the duties of getting the children up and ready for school, giving baths, washing dishes, and changing and fixing

Kimberly's bottle and feeding her I still had time to play

baseball on a team and catch garter snakes with my cousin Joshua.

My grades were still good and I was playing on a baseball team with teammates that were at least 2 years older than I was. I played second base and I loved it. It was the place where I go and not have any worries about what my parents were doing or getting called to do something by my grandmother or some other person. This is the time that made me and my cousin Joshua's best friends although I did have to share that with his other best friend, Keith, who was arguably the best player on the team and was always at the top of any sport he played. These are two people I looked up to at the time. Keith was pitcher or shortstop and Joshua was our center fielder and coach Rod was the best coach in the league. I pray he rest in peace.

Even though this year was one of my best years personally the family did have to deal with tragedy to my immediate blood family. My Aunt Linda had been gunned down and shot in the head from point-blank range with a $20 bill balled up in her hand. She had stopped doing drugs for about five years up until then. So it was a shock to the family to not just find out that she had been shot, but to find out that it was over drugs. This brought our family closer together while we all tried to process our feelings.

The next year we moved again, back to the same area that I lived with my grandfather. I was back in the same area where my mom met my step-father. The first place I moved to after being born. Everything had come back full circle as I was in the fifth grade, back at Spaulding elementary school where the principal offered my mom an opportunity to allow

me a double promotion because I was doing so well in school. I was doing so well that I would finish my work and have enough time to be the class clown, help others with their work, and daydream, but my mom turned him down and I remember my little heart being so devastated.

I held resentment towards my mother for many, many years for this one decision, one that she didn't and still doesn't remember. That and the time when I was walking home from school that year and found a real gold ring that had an "R" initial in it in cursive. It was so beautiful and the first person I could think of was my mother. Because I was a child that was oblivious to other people's faults I took the ring right in, with a big smile on my face and gave it right to my mom, just to find that a few days later she had "lost" it.

We started my sixth-grade year at the same place

surprisingly but did end up moving with my grandfather in the Miller area, which is a beach area in Gary, Indiana. He was living by himself on his retirement from the steel mill. My Aunt Renee, now, many years removed from doing drugs had been taking care of him. Her son, my cousin Sidney had been living with and taking care of him, so my family and I moved in with them.

My grandfather was now in a wheelchair and was unable to take care of himself so my mom and Sidney took care of his daily necessities. Although he was in this condition he had more life and was much happier than I had ever remembered him. He always puts a smile on my face. My nickname was Boo-man, but to him, I was Boo-man-chu with respect for baseball players that wore the Manchu mustache. He was a lifelong Dodgers fan since Jackie Robinson and the Brooklyn

Dodgers. I'm happy my Uncle Louis was able to take him to a Dodgers game before he died. When I saw pictures he looked like he was already in heaven.

My sixth-grade year was also a great year because I won a championship as the star pitcher of my 11-12-year-old baseball team. It was a game where we were the underdogs because the team we were up against had won more games that year during the season than we did and they had more stars on their team than we did. It was the quintessential game where the underdog takes down the giant in great fashion. They were up to bat in the bottom of the ninth and they were down by only as much as two points with runners in scoring position and me on the mound. I was known for a cutting fastball that not many people could hit and I was pitching the whole game. It was a low scoring game. I wasted no time getting the last out with two balls; I threw three strikes, back to back to back! Ball game! It was over. We had won the championship and nobody could take that away. My parents weren't there, but I was congratulated by my teammates and the neighborhood gangsters, who always would tell me, especially on this day, to stay out of the streets, and let baseball take me away. That wisdom sticks with me, even now. It was the best day of my young life.

The next year, the family, all 10 of us moved back in with granny, after my mom's dad passed away. It was a very somber funeral, but everyone accepted his passing away because we knew that although he was happy, he didn't like being limited to a wheelchair and having people serve his every need. My grandfather was a very proud man that had

been completely humbled by life so he didn't like being a a burden to others anymore.

Living at grannies was very different this time around because I was now an official teenager and there were many changes taking place within me. For one I was more self-conscious. I was also looking at my place in the world and

was noticing women and girls a lot more in ways that made me get happy in places that didn't get happy before. It was a whole new world and my attitude showed it. I would get upset and resent granny for calling my name so much, even though I still forced myself to do what she asked. I had distanced myself from my mom and dad and stayed as far away from them as I could, but they always seemed to call my damn name to do things like go to the store and buy them cigarettes or take my brothers and sisters to the park. It was so annoying. All I wanted to do was watch TV, go to the park when I wanted to, and not be bothered.

I was even getting frustrated with baseball at the time. After I and my team had won the championship, I was recruited to come and play in a more competitive league and I didn't like the fact that most of the team already had positions on the team and I was expected to just come in and take what was left without competing. This disheartened me and was a major hit to my confidence and self-esteem. I felt emotions very deeply, but I always disregarded them. So I played on without the passion that I had before and it showed on the field, even though I did hit the go-ahead run in our victory, off the bench, to land us 4th in the state of Indiana with my 13-15yr old team. There are newspaper clippings on this team. It was a great run for an inner-city team that was counted out.

Shining through Darkness | 19

My seventh and eighth-grade years were a time of change. I didn't care as much as I used to, about pretty much anything. The years of being around so much negativity were now taking its toll on me in the form of less energy, self- doubt, the anxiety that teetered on the side of paranoia, and depression, but I was too young to notice at the time and I still had to take care of the home, go to school and play baseball.

I did make the National Junior Honor Society and was transferred to the Academically Advanced classes which were amazing rewards for the work that I had put in up until that time. My teachers were excited for me and did their best to keep me encouraged which is the only reason why I think my grades were still pretty good during my final year of middle school. Thank you to those teachers at Dunbar-Pulaski Middle School. My glory days of being academically astute were sadly, but truly coming to an end.

My high school years were spent at West Side High. The home of the Cougars! Once again the family and I had moved to the west side of Gary to the Concord Homes, another low-income housing area. Most of the guys that I had played baseball with were going to the same school so the transition wasn't like the times when I had moved and gone to a school where I didn't know anyone. These years were filled with all types of twists and turns.

During my freshman year, I spent most of my time half-ass doing my work and sleep in the classrooms. I was just mindlessly going through the motions from home to school, and baseball games and practices. It was very sad and uninspiring as I look back. All of my friends and seemingly every other person in my school seemed to have it all figured out and was

enjoying themselves to the max and I was walking around wondering why and how could I have what they had. Talk about confused.

My sophomore year was a little more upbeat! This is the year where I managed to date a girl, very smart, courageous and had an amazing physique. We dated for 2 months max, but she did meet the family and she wasn't scared off. Impressive. I also tried out and made the Track & Field team where I was one of the fastest people on the team, earning me a spot on the 4x100 meter team where my best time was a 9.9 split. I even managed to make the honor roll in one of the marking periods. I also got my first job ever right after I finished school that year. It was a summer job filing paper and answering the phone. I don't know where this came from, but it was much needed.

My junior year was much different. My mother had run away to San Diego with one of my siblings. While she was at the bus station she called me and told me that she had to leave to get her life together and that my Uncle Louis and Aunt Theresa was going to help her get on her feet. On one hand, I understood, but on the other, I knew that I would have to deal with my step-father on my own and I would have more responsibility with my siblings. I was heart-broken even more. Even though I had deep resentments towards my mom there was still always some type of connection that I couldn't break.

Maybe this is why I lashed out and began coming home whenever I wanted to and smoking weed and skipping class. I think it was a combination of being a teen almost out of high school and being fed up, so I was kicked out of the house.

Some of the baseball moms knew a little bit about what was going on in my life so one of them allowed me to move in with my friend DeAndre and his family. It felt right because it was mostly men and they had what I believed to be a "real" family. The parents went to work and supported the children and the children were able to have the freedom to be children. Sadly enough I found a way to get kicked out by skipping school and bringing my girlfriend to the house and stupidly have sex in the parents' bed. I wouldn't have gotten caught if I hadn't of left whip cream in the bedroom causing the wife to question the husband. Silly me.

So, I moved back home to find that my step-father had been going to narcotics anonymous classes and attending culinary arts school which had taken his focus and attention away from the drugs. I was proud of him. He had also been recognized for father of the year by the city of Gary at our baseball teams' award ceremony for being a single dad. Meanwhile, things at school were still up and down, but I was in a much better place energetically. I had stopped track and field but continued to be one of the best players on our baseball team. I had a girlfriend that I got into a lot of trouble with, even though I thought it was fun.

My senior year was spent skipping classes, spending time with my girlfriend, gambling in the high school bathrooms, and smoking weed. I had mentally checked out of school even though I still went. Needless to say, I didn't play baseball that year, but the good news is that my mom did come back that year.

My mom had come back a new woman. She had gone down to San Diego, spent time in jail where she had a lot of time to contemplate and realize that she had to live and do better for her children. This was her motivation to come back. She may or may not have considered the backlash she would get from us and my step-father's family, but she came back, withstood it and stayed firmly away from reverting to drugs.

She had to also deal with the fact that my step-father did start back doing drugs due in large part to the fact that he had been diagnosed with a flesh-eating disease called scleroderma which is akin to lupus. This was an extremely painful disease which all of his children and family members watched him go through day by day until he passed away in March 2005, a few days before his birthday. May my step-father, Rhymuless Darnell Lenoir be forgiven all his transgressions as I pray he, too, rests in peace. I'm thankful for the lessons that I learned later in life through him.

When my mom came back, though, she brought another addition to the family, a baby sister named Skylah. Beautiful and vibrant, she stole the hearts of everyone she came in contact with including granny and my step-father. She was an irresistibly passionate, and talented little girl and a breath of fresh air for everyone. She made everybody light up.

This was the start of a new era. After I completed

my high school credits in summer school after my senior year, my mom came back, Skylah came, and my stepfather died so I figured it was time for me to move. I looked for jobs around the area but wasn't successful because my life's journey had other plans, so the job I took was a traveling job. So at the age of

19 I bid farewell to my family and headed out towards Orlando, Florida.

Dark Days at Home

I know we're going forward, but before we do that, I want

to take you inside the house where I was so you can see the
depths from which I had to work my way out to
balance the dark with the light. We all know that my parents
were addicted to crack cocaine and we all know that Gary,
Indiana was the murder capital of the United States of
America, but what was going on inside were the dark days at
home. I hope you're not afraid to see because it's about to
get real.

As I mentioned before, my step-father wasn't just dealing
crack, but he was also doing it, meaning he had many
"friends" to do them with. As a young boy, I would have
laughed with these friends of theirs, running around as we all
listened to the music that my parents were playing. That is
until they all decided to leave me and my sister, Candis, in the

living room as they would all go downstairs to the "grown-up"
room.

From there, a strong, foul smell would sweep up into the
living room turning mine and my sister's face sour and
making my stomach turn over and over again. They would
stay downstairs for as long as they could talking and laughing
until I guess the crack set in and made them all come
out back upstairs. When they would come up their faces
would be shaped in many different ways, and their eyes had

no life and seemed very distant. They would all leave outside where some would stay close to the house and others would walk away into the distance.

The more and more my parents went away on their own or with their friends the more and more I would feel the change. My mother had become more distant from me and my step-father snapped at me a lot quicker. I also saw the friends that used to come around a lot begin to come around less and less. Even when our parents did spend time with us, the children, it was a very anxiety-ridden time, yet the fact is we were just happy to have our parents with us.

It seemed as if, now looking back, that the more they went and got high with each other the more children came about. It also seemed that the more children that they had, the more they relied on the drugs. It was a ridiculously vicious cycle that no child should have to go through. This was and is my life. I wouldn't change it for the world. The world is what had put me in this predicament in the first place and what I've come to realize is that I can't overcome what the world had for me no matter how hard I try. So I just go with it and make the best out of whatever situation is in front of me.

26 | BALANCING DARK WITH LIGHT

As I got older the dynamics inside the house got more and more intense. The personality that my step-father would display when high was extreme paranoia. He and my mom would go into the room and when he was high enough he would burst through the door and turn off the first light that he saw. For some reason, he liked for the house to be dark. He would go from room to room, like an army soldier in a war hiding behind every wall continuously turning off light after light scaring the shit out of the children.

While he was playing Rambo, sometimes with a knife in his hand, my mother would be frozen in a corner. Her personality was the scared and distressed type, which was lost and just didn't know what to do. She would twist her lips and twirl her toes while asking my step-father "why are you doing this?"

Meanwhile, I would be holding whoever the baby was at the time as we, the children were all cornered together moving out of the way whenever he would come our way. He wouldn't even say anything sometimes and just seem as though he was looking right through us. I had been used to it at this point, but the others were terrified.

He would also turn over pillows on our couches and search in the seams, I guess to see if there were any crack baggies inside of them. Whenever he did find something similar, he would put it up to his mouth to eventually spit it out. While this is all happening, my mom would look as if she was being tortured by whatever was going on in her mind and that was the scariest thing for me.

Dark Days at Home | 27

There would be times where he would grab me and take me from window to window, I guess as a form of protection from whatever he thought was chasing him. He would ask me, "why would you do this to me," and "see what you did." For the record, I had no idea what he was talking about. Maybe it was deeper than what I could see at the time.

While he was going from window to window with me under one arm, in the other hand, would be that knife that I told you about. He would have gallons of sweat running down his face, while saying that there was a"monkey" in the tree in which at this time, my siblings now being a little older and used to this would respond, by asking each other, "Do you see a monkey in the tree, because I don't see a monkey in the tree."

It was funny, but more to them than to me because I had a paranoid drug addict parent holding a knife close to my neck and walking around asking if we could see things that didn't exist. Oh my God! We were all confused.

On nights like this, we all had to stay up and be a part of this movie, that wasn't a movie, but our actual life, while other children were at home probably getting a good night's rest or at least disobeying their parents by staying up and listening to music or watching TV, before getting up and going to school

the next day. That's just how we rolled. Apparently, right?
As he calmed down and they went to their room or left out
again in the middle of the night that would finally give us a
chance to get some sleep. I would hold whichever the baby
was and feed them their bottle and help whichever one of

them that needed some kind of help and we would all fall
asleep, exhausted from a very action-packed night.

The next morning I would have to get school clothes
ready, walk the youngest siblings to school before
coming back and waking my mom up to take care of the baby
before I left for school myself.

Some of my other duties were giving baths to the boys as
Candis would do the same for the girls. I also was in charge
of washing the dishes, washing clothes, getting school clothes
ready, dressing the boys and sometimes the girls, waking all
the kids up, and going back and forth to the store for our
family needs. Not to mention, being step-dads protection
against spooky spirits.

There was also this one time when after getting higher than
the moon my step-dad was wondering why we were setting
him up to be taken away. This belief was so real to him that
in the middle of December in the midwest he decided to open
our door, make us put on shoes and put us all outside. He

didn't spare anyone because he even put my mother out. We were shocked, but probably more cold than anything! After getting over that initial fear and shock

the cold set in and overruled everything so we surely made our way back in that house. Who does that!?

I bet the crack dealers didn't know this type of shit happened or they did and just didn't care. I don't blame them because there's enough blame to go around from the mindset of our ancestors, to my parents, to the drug dealers, and of course the United States government. It's up to us to break the cycles. One by one, person by person.

Florida, New Beginnings

Now it was time for me to see what the world had to offer outside of Gary, Indiana. I was still full of fear, worries, and resentments, but I was on a brand new journey. This journey in particular was of a proud, brand new, and fresh off the press door to door salesman of your favorite magazines or magazines you didn't know anything about, but you definitely needed to subscribe.

I traded in my family, sadly, even my brothers and sisters, for a traveling organization that stopped in every inner city to recruit any young adult that was seeking some type of change in their life. This organization took children of the American ghettos and brought them door to door and face to face with some of the most affluent neighborhoods and people in America.

30 | BALANCING DARK WITH LIGHT

I had no idea what I was getting myself into or what this the organization was all about until I found myself waking up on one of a few vans in the beautiful, sunny city of Orlando, Florida! I was pleasantly surprised and scared out of my mind because I had never been this far away from home.

I was real reserved around other people for the simple fact that I didn't trust humans at all. I didn't care how charismatic they were or how cool they were, but the more they showed me how open and "real" they were the more I opened up and showed how awkward I was.

I truly didn't know how to express myself at this time. I constantly thought about what others expected of me because I didn't have any expectations for myself. I was consistently hard on myself and was terrified to speak in front of people, no matter if it was one on one or in front of many people because I didn't want to say anything wrong that would piss someone off and makes them mad at me. I wanted them to continue liking me, probably because I didn't really like myself.

All of these were just a few of the feelings that I felt even though at the time I was living and had no idea if any of these concepts whatsoever. I was oblivious of what was going on inside of me because that was just a place that I did not go! The owners of this organization were older, the mid-50s or early 60s African American married couple. As I remember they were a very beautiful couple whose hearts were in the right place, helping themselves by helping others. They explained to us that they had drivers that would drive us to these nice areas where we would go door to door and

say this pitch, one I can't remember right now, but we had to make sure to do it with personality, while having fun with it. They then had some of the veterans get upfront and show us, rookies, how it was done. I was thoroughly impressed by how much confidence they had.

On our way out, on the van, a few of the people that had been there a while began sharing with me that if I was lucky then I could hit the "jackpot" like some of the others that had come and sold magazines before. The "jackpot" was finding a sugar mama that would let me move into their gigantic house and take care of me where all I would have to do is give them some of my good, hood loving to keep them satisfied. I seriously considered this information.

What's funny is that I had an opportunity present itself to me.

I was out one day doing my door to door thing when all of a sudden rain began to pour down. I had received a call that my ride was about an hour away, so I was standing outside getting drenched when a woman and her son, maybe a middle or high school kid pulled up and asked if I was okay. I told her the situation and she asked me if I wanted to come in and dry off before I was to get picked up. Of course, I said yes. I was getting drenched for crying out loud.

As I go in she asks me if I would like to put on some of her ex-husband's clothes while I dry off. I declined the offer. Then she left and let me know that I could get a drink if I wanted while she tended to her son. She got her son ready and then

went to tuck him in for the night. As she came out she was wearing a night robe as she asked me if my ride would be showing up anytime soon and offered to take me home if I needed, but being the naïve young person with no sense of what 19yr olds from the hood would do, I declined and told her that my ride would be there soon as I left and went outside. I'm still a tad bit ashamed of this story.

As we finished out the night and we all got back to the hotel almost everyone gathered up in one of the co-worker's room. We gathered in their room because they were the people that everyone got their weed from. They had family close by so they had the Florida connection. It was a couple and this was their side hustle. We didn't mind because we didn't have to go out and we could just get what we needed from one of ours. This is where everybody would talk about their day; listen to music and freestyle.

This experience had already been showing positive signs. It was entertaining and fun, but damn, my feet hurt. That didn't stop me though because I was seeing how much money I was making and I didn't have to worry about where my next meal was coming from or if I would have to deal with the stress of having someone come in and intrude on my space.

There was another time where I went out and had come across a couple that probably should have been born during Woodstock in the 60's because their house was so bright and vibrant, and their demeanor was so relaxed and laid back that it was easy to feel comfortable around them. They then decided to invite me into their home after I gave them my pitch with my charming charisma. As they invited me in I made sure there was no weird sex talk being had at all, and to my surprise, all they wanted to do was let me see their house and ask if I smoked weed. I immediately said yea and they begin telling their political beliefs on marijuana and how if people had a joint a day then the world would be a much better. They also, while we were smoking their bong, schooled me on the strain of weed and how good it was. I must say, that was some really good weed and I'm sure I didn't say a word and just listened, smiled and nodded the whole time.

I finally left after spending a large part of my day hanging out with them, afterwards leaving to walk around their now, even more beautiful neighborhood. Of course, it was after they purchased a subscription of whatever magazine they chose, probably one about marijuana. I had to do it! Wink wink.

As you can see there was never a dull moment in the amazing world of selling magazines door to door. There were awkward moments, fun, random moments, but also scary, random moments like the time that I almost got shot and eaten by a dog. This might be a little dramatic but check out the next story.

I was in Orlando, but it was still the south, and I don't know if you've realized yet, but I was a young black man in a neighborhood that more than likely didn't have many people that looked like me. They especially didn't have as much swagger, no matter how much insecurities the swagger was covering up.

I'm just minding my business serving people these magazines when I walk up to a house that had someone open the blinds, look out and close them real quick. It was weird,

yes, but not weird enough to stop me from getting my money, so I continued up the walkway. As I continued up I hear a dog barking and then I see a man that happened to be white standing behind a glass door with a shotgun saying, if you don't get off my property I'll shoot you and send my dog out to clean up the remains. So yeah, I ran off his property as fast as possible letting him know that he could kiss my black ass.

A week had gone by; actually, six days of going out for hours at a time and finally an off day came about. This day we could do what we wanted and explore the city. But not before everyone was acknowledged and awarded with their checks for the hard-work and new records, if any, had been accomplished.

I was tired, but because I was a person that didn't know his boundaries and would always keep moving I had done better than some of the people that had been there and was also acknowledged for coming close to the record for selling the most magazine subscriptions in the first week in the organizations history. Also, the check was pretty damn nice.

So after the meeting, I went to the couple, bought my weed and went out to explore Orlando with some of the guys that I met. While out I realized that even though I was doing pretty well, I was tired of working six days a week and it was too much for me because I couldn't be lazy like I was used to.

I also remembered that my Uncle Louis was in Florida so I got his contact from my mom and called him to see if I could move in with him and he said yes! I was stoked, so when I got

back to the hotel, I informed the male owner of my decision and he did everything he could to keep me, but eventually he let me go. So the next day I was on a bus, headed to a place named Niceville, Florida, a military city where my uncle was preparing to retire from the Navy after 22 years.

I met my uncle once before now heading to live with him and was reminded of the time when he came to check on me and Candis after my mom left because we weren't blood-related. Of course, this moment ended in an argument and almost a fight between my step-dad and my uncle. My uncle yelled out that I had a family that loved me and we could move with them if we wanted. At that time, my step-dads was the only family, my sister and I knew. She wanted to stay for that reason and to an extent, I did too, but I knew for sure that I had to stay for my siblings.

I didn't know what to expect nor did I have any expectations because for one I wasn't wired to look ahead and number two I had nothing to go off of that would give me an idea of what to expect. One thing I did find out when I got there is that this was a time in my life that would require me to have some form of discipline because as I mentioned before, my uncle was a 22-year military man and discipline was his middle name. Lord help me!

My uncle not just disciplined, but he's analytical, intellectual, hard-working, and to my surprise a lot of fun. He let me have one maybe two days to rest before he rushed into the room he let me use and asked me what was it that I was doing to find work to which I replied, something to the effect of, I'm still waking up. From there he cursed my ass out

and put me out of his house to go and start filling out applications.

As I began searching, less than one week later I got a response from the least likely of places for a person coming from my background, Panera Bread. This is a place that I had never had contact with. I knew nothing about bread bowls or what a Panini was, but it turned out to be exactly what I needed. This was a place completely outside of my realm of knowledge.

The employees were weird and awkward, the customers were weird and awkward, and they were also white believe it or not. I was in a whole new world of weird, awkward people and I fit right in.

This was the first time I had ever met surfers because I was close to Destin, Florida, or heard of folk music, let alone hearing it and it was also my first-time hearing of someone doing a drug called mushrooms. I had heard of the food mushrooms and I didn't like those so I was pretty sure I wouldn't like the drug for that and other obvious reasons like the fact that I was really closed minded.

Not only did I work at Panera Bread, but I also worked at a nightclub as a bouncer. The name of the club was The Swamp. They played live rock and roll music, another first for me, and they had a DJ who plays hip-hop and pop for the college students, beach bodies, and visitors from other countries to go wild. This is when the story gets very interesting. Enter playboy Anthony.

I was the only black guy there with the background that I had, I was young, around 22, pretty handsome, and a lot of

pent up frustrations. I didn't care about anything. I
also had my own place and my car at this time. From
my point of view, at that time, it was a young man's dream.
I'll share an intense story with you.

Our club had two levels to it and after a certain time, we would
close the upstairs and channel everyone in the club
downstairs. This particular night I had duties to oversee the
dance floor from upstairs. As I was looking around the dance
floor checking everything out I locked eyes with an exchange
student from Russia. Her name was Olga or something
Russian like that. She was dancing and moving very sensually
while looking right at me, so I left my post and went
downstairs and walked directly to her and asked her if she
wanted to join me upstairs. She obliged.

As we make it to the stairs, I grab her hand as we go up, I
lead her to a back exit area where no one was and began
passionately locking lips with her as my hands grab and caress
almost every inch of her body. Before turning her around,
now kissing her neck and rubbing her breasts while playing
with her nipples. Just as I feel that she's completely turned on,
I bend her over, snap her thong and enter her ever so gently
before sliding back and thrusting forward again and again,
holding her by her waist as she holds herself up against the
the wall I gently grab her long beautiful hair right before I

explode and let go of all the pent up frustrations that had been held back for far too long.

This and other stories like this are what my life was like at this time. They may not be the most tasteful, but they are true and I enjoyed every one of them the best way I could at the time. No, she did not end up pregnant, but she did tell two of

her Russian friends about our night then and at my apartment. Somehow, someway, they both found me and made sure that they tested some of the emotionally unstable black guy from Gary, Indiana.

The club didn't only bring sexual situations my way, and plenty of them, it also brought me and my uncle closer together. Which is the reason why I said he was surprisingly fun? He showed me how to have fun whenever I went out. I guess partying with women was something that he was able to master during his 22 years of traveling the world. That's one of the many feats he conquered in addition to helping to battle and secure "American interests" in the Gulf War. Anyway, that's not where this story is going, but I felt it had to be said.

One night, while out with my uncle I met a guy named Dan. Dan was from Jersey and had come upon some money, deciding to move and retire to Florida at the ripe old age of

25. Dan and I hit it off, probably because his birthday just so happens to be the same as mine. I think we gave each other something to do besides always going out to a club.

Don't mix it up, we did go out, pretty much every weekend, but not just that. We'd go to the beach and throw the football around, show off, and flirt with the girls, then go to his house, smoke the best weed, watch football, eat and talk shit. We were two peas in a pod. Wherever you saw one you were sure to see the other unless we brought girls home because in that case, we were in our rooms doing our things.

Speaking of doing our things, I also had jobs, after the other two, at Kmart, and a family-owned grocery store. There are other stories of me, women and the workplace that I could share, but this isn't the time or place for any more of those stories. Let's talk about how hard-working and stable I had become. At least it looked that way on the outside. I had my place, my car, a clean 1986 Mercury Grand Marquis, and two jobs that I worked hard at.

One day at Kmart a few firemen came in and as soon as I saw them I walked over and asked them what I could do to become a fireman like them and they told me that I would have to go to school for 6 months. They then gave me some information and I looked it up as soon as I got the opportunity.

After looking it up and finding out the tuition fee I
asked my uncle to pay it for me and we came up with a payment
plan so that I could pay him back in the quickest time
possible. As soon as the money hit my account I enrolled
in Gulf Coast Community college. This was a new challenge
and I was determined and ready.

When I began the class there were two black men, me and
a younger guy from Ft. Lauderdale and there was one white
woman, the rest of the 20 were all white men. This is
something that I noticed, but it didn't phase me, it actually
acted as fuel for me.

I enjoyed it. There were mental tests that included
reading and writing. There were physical tests that were
also mentally challenging and something that I was good at.
I was going for something that anyone else would want to stay

away from. Finally! There was something good that I could
take from my childhood. Being cool in the middle of a fire.
We had to crawl through smoke-filled buildings and rescue
dummies that were over 100lbs. We had to learn how to tie
certain knots with ropes and then climb ladders and tie the
knots while under distress. We also had to bust car windows
with small pens and use the Jaws of Life to cut off car doors.

These were all things that I had fun doing and I did them all very well. Not everyone made it to this point and others weren't able to make it past this point. Although I was rooting for everyone, I was sure proud to be one of the people that were still around.

One of the happiest days of my life was when it was all over and I got my certificate of recognition stating that I had done everything necessary to be acknowledged as a certified firefighter in the state of Florida. Not only that, I passed all the classes with an 85 point average!

I volunteered as a fireman for a while and continued to work enabling me to pay off my uncle. I also met a woman named Andrea who was older and she seemed like the final piece of my life. The glasses that I was wearing were rose-colored. I didn't see or care that she already had a daughter, she didn't have a car and she lived in a low-income community. I fully trusted her with no evidence to do such a mindless thing. I figured that since her sister had money that she had money too. I was young and dumb, but I was many years removed from being a high school kid.

During my time with her, I found out that I wasn't able to practice as a fireman until I had attained an Emergency Medical Technicians certificate along with my fireman's certification. She came into my life in the middle of my schooling during which I decided to move out of my apartment to move in with her. I fully trusted her and I had no reason to do so.

I later found out that she was writing and cashing checks from my account. Even though I would come up short on some bills, I never knew until I went through my book of checks and saw my name in her handwriting. She was at home when I left for work and at home when I got home from work. Her story was that she had helped her sister and that's where she got her money. I was extremely gullible. Green is what some people would call it, but my greens were neon though. Very light!

She also told me that she was pregnant with my child. I was scared and shocked and had many other emotions and feelings come up after hearing that I would be a father at 23 years of age. I excitedly told the news to my mom and co-workers. My co-workers decided to set up a baby shower for us. It was at a park and it turned out nice. Very interesting. Her doctor's appointments were always on days that I had to work which was okay with me. She would tell me about the progress and it would make me smile because now I was happy that I was going to be a father, sparking me to begin thinking about marriage.

She was a little chubby so up until this time I hadn't taken into consideration that she wasn't getting much bigger. So at

42 | BALANCING DARK WITH LIGHT

this time I began doing my research and ended up at her doctor's office grilling him and demanding that he give me information. Of course, he could not. I contacted her sister and she told me that I needed to take that up with her. Then Andrea finally came to me and told me that she was never pregnant and that she was sorry and understood if I wanted to leave her.

She was right! I was out of there the next morning, staying with one of my co-workers and her son who introduced me to some trippy, but extremely creative music.Mushrooms! The point is that it was time to move on to the unknown. So after staying with my co-worker whose name is One, pronounced (oh-nee) for a little while I prepared to move once again with my Uncle Louis, this time to Houston, Texas.

Houston Life

Thank God for Uncle Louis! Now retired from the military, he decided to spend his retirement working at the Home Depot. He could never just sit around, he always had to be on the go. So when I arrived he made sure I was looking for work on day one! He didn't have to worry too much this time because I had learned from the first time he took in a stray nephew.

I was searching and searching and putting out application after application to no avail. I was still in a funk though so I wasn't putting out the right energy to obtain a new job. I was putting out applications, but I wasn't putting in enough effort. The fact is that I wasn't moving my body. I was just sitting behind a computer just going through the motions without any true intent.

44 | BALANCING DARK WITH LIGHT

My uncle noticed that I wasn't making any real progress and probably noticed that I was still in a dark place, whether I knew it or not, so he reluctantly put in a good word where he was working and because of his power I was hired to work in the lumber department at the same Home Depot.

I was on my way! I had a comfortable place to rest, a family member that loved me dearly in his way, which I took for granted on more than one occasion, and a stable job with a 401k, something I had never even heard of. I didn't even care what it was, I just knew that it saved an extra $3 per hour for me and accumulated along a period and I was all for it.

Although I had put myself in a position where I had lost my job, my apartment, and for better or worse, my girlfriend by the irresponsible and boneheaded decisions that I had made I still ended up in a pretty good situation, in a completely different part of the country.

I, at that time, couldn't see the forest for the trees, probably because I had no depth which in turn provided me with no appreciation. So I just went to work and came home with no sense of direction and no sense of adventure.

Enter my co worker Jason, a very handsome ladies' man that had no lack of self-confidence and walked around like a superstar. So much so that he would walk into work at least 30 minutes late every single day. No exaggeration. And they let him do it, which was an amazing thing.

This guy was my age, worked in the same department where we became good friends. He didn't have a problem

with adventure, but was just as bad as me when it came to a sense of direction. Needless to say, it was time for some adventures.

He went to the University of Houston and from what I gathered was pretty well known. The guys liked him and the girls adored him. The way that I found that out as he would sneak me inside whenever we wanted to go play some people on the basketball court. We would spend the first hour or two just walking around socializing. He was self-confident and it was cool to see because I was nothing like that.

 Then we would eventually end up on the basketball court where he had what I call a "pretty boy" game, meaning he would shoot mid-range and 3 pointers and I would shoot mid-range and go to the basket. We played well together. We would also find ourselves going out and hitting the town together. I didn't know people or talk much and he knew everybody and talked too much. I would find myself solo just observing before he came back around. Again something else that was very interesting for me to watch. I felt pretty jealous because in my head I thought I was as cool as he was displaying. I was supposed to be having fun, but those were sad days for the insecure Anthony.

Although nightlife wasn't my strong suit I did pretty well at my job. I was reliable during dependent matters as you can see, but I was the worst when it came to me being independent and having to go get something myself. Only if I knew then what I know now, right? The fact is I wouldn't change one thing.

Anyway, I worked for the Home Depot for about a year before I remembered that I had to have a certificate in Emergency Medical Services to become a firefighter and so I began researching until I found classes at Houston Community College and enrolled. To my surprise, it would only take me 3 months to finish the course so I started as soon as possible.

In this class, I learned many very important ways to save and maintain a person's life, like taking blood pressure and knowing what a stable blood pressure was and the proper procedure for CPR and so forth. I also learned that no call that I would respond to would ever be the same and that some calls would be a learning experience that one would never want to be taught.

Our instructor was very knowledgeable in medical services, had many years of experience. He was a great teacher and shared one of these horrific stories. He also had a pretty dark sense of humor that I came to appreciate. He told us of a time when he was on a run and he came up to a man's home. He noticed that the man was continually moving around frantically and as our teacher proceeded to ask him what the problem was. The man yelled out "it's still alive" and dumbfounded, my professor, asked him what was still alive.

Come to find out this man had a fetish where he would put a gerbil in his anus where the gerbil was supposed to die and vibrate giving him a sensation in his anus that would get him off. Sadly this time around we know it was "still alive." So yeah, I learned a lot in my EMT class and passed my state test above 80%.

This was amazing. Although I wasn't able to work as a fireman because my certifications were in two different states, I was able to work as an EMT and since Houston had more than 300 private and public owned services, finding a job would be no problem. So to celebrate my uncle took me to Onyx strip club where I had a ball and was able to see another side of Uncle Louis. I really can't put a feeling on how I felt about that. I just wanted the alcohol to keep flowing.

I was now about to begin working on an ambulance, something that I never thought I would be doing. Here I am about to go out and save lives! At least that's what I imagined in my head. Most of the privately-owned services were transport services for dialysis patients. I was a little saddened by this fact for a while, but what made me overcome that quickly was the fact that I was going to get paid more than I ever had before and I could work for two companies at a time. As I was transporting patients and making good money I began to notice that I was taking the same people back and forth each week naturally causing me to build a relationship with them and sometimes their families. The patients I was transporting were usually elderly people in their 60s or older. Some were amputees and the others were just extremely weak so we had to make sure that their blood pressure was up to par and their mental status was stable unless the patient had dementia which wasn't that rare.

We became so close that family members would invite us to birthday parties where we would meet their spouse of 50yrs which was very impressive to me. Or the families would invite us to the patients' funeral which didn't happen that often, but made me sad nonetheless.

48 | BALANCING DARK WITH LIGHT

Transporting the older patients had a place in my heart, but not as much as the times when I had to transport the children. The children's transports were tough for me because they were so innocent, yet they were going through some type of severe pain or suffering. Sometimes you would want to fight the parents because you would just feel that something was going on, but there was nothing we could do. There were also the young cancer patients that would need to be taken to a specialized cancer hospital.

There was one instance where we had arrived at a young

Latino family's home and I noticed how distraught the mother and grandmother were making me think that one of them was the patient because the little boy had a smile on his face and a sense of wonder. He helped me to feel comfortable. As we got on the ambulance I made sure I got his vitals as he settled in. The mom was riding along so I made sure she was secure and comfortable as well and I began talking to the little boy. I found out his name and his age and that he had been diagnosed with cancer since he was around four years old. He was now six. So to keep his spirits up I made him a turkey out of a latex glove which I had learned from a veteran a week before. He lit up and enjoyed an otherwise scary time before we turned him happily over to the staff at the hospital.

These are the moments that made my job feel special. I had no expectations from any of my patients but they always showed appreciation even if I was afraid to accept it. The cool thing is that one week later, I walked into work and my supervisor called me into his office and handed me a pink letter from the mom of the young boy with his picture in it,

stating how well he was doing and inviting me to have a meal with the family whenever I wanted. I still have that letter to this day to remind me that every life is precious so make every moment around them count.

Life was going pretty great at this point. I had gotten my own apartment, this time with furniture and a big screen, I had a nicer car and I had a beautiful Nigerian girlfriend named Esther with the body of a goddess.

I met her during her birthday weekend at a bar/restaurant, yeah she loved to have a drink and that was the perfect time for her and me. She was getting ready to leave and I was standing outside thinking to myself that there was no way I was going to let her leave without me talking to her. So I went over, stopped her from getting in the car and made sure everything was on point so she couldn't do anything but give me her contact information.

She lived an hour away in Beaumont, Texas and was attending Lamar University where she was studying speech pathology to help children with speech impediments. I told you all that children held a special place in my heart so when I found that out it made me want to take and make a baby with her right there. Well, I wanted to at least practice making a baby anyway.

She was highly dramatic and so was I making for a very passionate and toxic relationship, but I loved it. She knew how to make me go crazy and I did the same. We were young and in love and it showed because we spent so much time with each other.

We did everything together from cooking to going to clubs, attending weddings, and just enjoying nature. I met her mom, sisters, nephew, and brother. She met Uncle Louis and my biological father Alan. I had never felt for anyone like this before.

Yes, I met my dad, brother Alan Jr., sisters Amari and Amani while in Indiana while visiting home when I was living in Florida at the age of 22. My sister, Kashae', while taking his class, because he was a teacher at her high school, was informed, while he was passing out report cards that he "dated" my mom when they were younger, sparking my mom's memory, leading us to have a DNA test proving that he was my father. My relationship with him and the family has been good but distant ever since. Back to Esther.

I would wake up out of my bed in the middle of the night and drive to her just because she told me she missed me and felt lonely without me. Those were really good nights I must say. I wrote poems and dedicated songs to her I didn't know what love was, but I surely believed that this was it. Then things began to change. Story of my life, right?

I had been working as an EMT for four years and dating Esther for two. Everything was going just fine and dandy until one day, what seemed to be out of the blue: a monster truck full of thoughts and emotions smacked me right in the face. There was no more storage space inside of me to hold on to anything else. I was extremely overwhelmed and supremely outmatched.

The first signs of my instability showed up as me consistently being late for work because I couldn't sleep the night before.

Then I got into frequent disagreements and arguments with my colleagues. My relationship with my uncle and Esther were also suffering so much so that I had taken a break from both of them before using our great benefits at American Medical Response to seek help from a therapist, which didn't help at all. So I stopped going after the first session.

I got a new partner, a young, cute, white young lady, with blonde hair and a perky personality. I didn't care about my job so much that whenever we would have downtime at work she would meet me and we would find a place to go and have sex. Then, I had no concept that what I was doing was because I was pretty much in the middle of a mental breakdown. I don't regret it because I did learn from it.

Here we go again, right? Will I ever learn?

This was my fall from grace. After all this, I ended up quitting my job for no apparent reason, the engine in my car went out and I didn't have the money to fix it, Esther broke it off with me completely, and my uncle lost respect for me, but I was still, somehow, back on his couch after losing my apartment.

I was completely devastated. It all happened so fast. What was I going to do now?

My uncle did all he could to try to snap me out of it including cursing me the hell out and kicking me out, but all I did was crawl back feeling sorry for myself. It was only so much he could take after letting me back in before coming up with the plan to have me and his daughter Maria move into an apartment together.

52 | BALANCING DARK WITH LIGHT

My cousin Maria is a young vibrant, talented socialite, but saving money and being responsible were not her strong suits and I was pretty much going crazy. I became a failed drug dealer after smoking my entire weed stash and a failed escort after only going as far as putting my picture on an escort services website. Yes, please laugh at me because this is too ridiculous.

I spent my alone time between feelings of despair, sadness, resentment, anger, and reading self-help books about spirituality and the meaning of life and felt a strong passion for the unseen nature of life. I wanted to find out more, I would have to do it someplace else because I had run out of money and my uncle just couldn't take me back. So

Mom, Gary, Indiana, I'm sad to say it, but I'm coming back

home.

Faith, Resilience and Belief

Here I was, back in my old city, around the same buildings

that I grew up with. Now even more dilapidated than I could

remember. I had lost everything and was now back at ground

zero with my mom and her boyfriend Nate, a loud,

charismatic, act before you think the type of person who had just

spent over 10 years in prison. He wasn't a bad man, just

loud and obnoxious.

I had the idea to wait until my tax return came in and

getting back out on the road again, but to where I didn't know

at the moment. I didn't know much at that time, but I knew

I didn't want to stay and if I had to get a job it was going to be worth my time, but another problem is that there wasn't

much to choose from with the mindset that I had.

54 | BALANCING DARK WITH LIGHT

From there I went to the welfare office to apply for food

stamps. I told myself that I had paid enough into the system

to now be able to proudly take from the system. I guess it's

what I had to tell myself so I wouldn't have to face the fact

that I was humiliated and needed as much help as possible.

You know what, ignorant pride is fucking stupid.

I brought with me a few pairs of clothes and shoes and the

burning desire to figure out what the meaning of life was.

Especially now after seeing what losing all of my material

assets could do to a person. I was in a desperate place and all

I had to hold me up was my small understanding of

meditation and these books that I was now reading at the

local library. This new position I found myself in was

going to take some faith and resilience.

Even though I didn't have the most ideal upbringing,

the family made sure that all the children attended church almost

every Sunday. I'm pretty sure it was for deeply religious

reasons from our ancestors, but I'm also sure it was to get rid

of the kids for a few hours.

It was perfect for them because all they had to do was awake

us and make sure we were ready when the church bus

showed up and then send us out the door and on our way as fast as possible.

The church we went to for most of our childhood was called Fairhaven Baptist Church. It was a church that could get a person teased and humiliated by the bully and the bully him or herself to come and enjoy the lord. The church was in Chesterton, Indiana, a more country area with majority white people that sent buses out every Sunday to all the neighborhoods in Gary to bring them to church.

As a kid from our area, this was the place to go to have some fun and get out the hood for a while. They fed us, gave us opportunities to win prizes, let us run around and gave us a a safe place to sleep for a while on the bus.

A few of the ways to win prizes was to sing gospel songs the loudest, answer bible questions the most and bring as many guests as possible, which are all things I did pretty regularly. So much so that they had to consciously give prizes to other people to make it fair. Little did I know I was becoming more and more knowledgeable of the Bible by trying to win every single church competition there was. I even came close to attending their school, but what stopped me was the fact that my step-father tried to get the church people to pay him some money to have me attend. Yes, there was tuition to attend. What is life?

I learned as much as I could about the bible and did everything I could to believe in it, but what was happening in reality at home overpowered my belief. But, that didn't stop us from going to church.

As we got a little older we went to Aunt Renee's' church, Faith Tabernacle Deliverance Center. Faith Tabernacle Deliverance Center has a slick-talking, laid back preacher that looks like a pimp. At least that's what I thought when I was a kid. We also went to Allen Chapel C.M.E. church with a fire breathing preacher that ran an afterschool program and cursed too damn much.

I'm sure that these men loved Jesus in their way and did their best to spread the good news, but it just didn't work for me. Attending both of these churches was more entertaining with what was going on with the members of the church than the actual sermons preached. As I became more and more independent I moved further and further away from the church and Christianity in particular. I still had Jesus and the teachings within me, but I definitely wasn't able to deal with the church anymore.

But desperate times called for desperate measures so I went back to Allen Chapel. There was a new preacher, a

compassionate woman that seemed sincere. I could
listen to and retain the information that she was
putting out a lot of the sermons making sense concerning
my situation.

Going to church and reading the spiritual self-help books
were all helping me to have faith in something bigger than
my situation even though I still felt like the weight of the world
had come crumbling down on me.

I'm also reminded of the time when I attended a place
named The Church Without Walls in Houston. This was a
beautiful church with thousands of members, with many
outreach programs, nationally and internationally.

I enjoyed it because it just radiates positivity,
encouragement, action, and sincerity. The preacher there
was pretty real and didn't seem to hide much at all. I respect
that and would go back to this non-denominational church
for the experience alone.

My belief grew there, but even though I felt good
when I went and I was living well at the time the demons that
were inside of me continued to show their face and I wanted to
get rid of them completely and not cover them up with happy
thoughts and feelings.

These were also the same feelings and thoughts that I was

having as I continued day in and day out when I was reading all of the amazing books from my search for the meaning of life during my time in Houston and Indiana. This was all that I needed at the time though, no matter if it was a permanent or a temporary remedy.

I also remember when I was in Houston and I went to a a couple of Buddhist temples in an attempt to learn how to meditate. Going to church and my understanding of believing didn't seem to be helping me so now I wanted to see what meditation would do. I did that and I went to go and see a very deeply spiritual man that gave me some wisdom that helped me to have just a little more faith in something, but I didn't know what exactly.

Back in Gary, I continued to study, but I also had to try to find something to study that was a little more grounded. So I began reading books about acting! Not too grounded I guess. The plan had morphed into me getting my refund check and moving to San Diego with Aunt Theresa and her family before heading off to Los Angeles, California to pursue acting. I guess the reading was paying off in the form of overconfidence or just belief in myself. I was going to have to be resilient.

58 | BALANCING DARK WITH LIGHT

The main reason that I wanted to become an actor was to

come back and build up my community while making enough
money to do what I wanted to do. That was pretty deep. But
a deeper reason was that I wasn't satisfied with myself and
I didn't like who I was so I wanted to run as far away from
Anthony Vaughn as possible.

I had created many amazing ideas of how I would fix up my
city, but how could I get the resources to get into an acting
school that would put me in a better position to make this
newfound dream of mine come true?

Somehow I found out that Mayor Karen Freeman-Wilson
had an open-door policy to the citizens. Granny used to do
her hair when she was a little girl. She went to Harvard and
somehow had the ear of the President of the United States at
the time, Mr. Barack Obama.

I found all of this information by talking to granny and
researching on the library computer. I also researched
information on the history of Gary, Indiana finding that this
city used to be a well-oiled machine, but was now really run
down and in the deficit brought on by Mayors with the right
intentions but the wrong ideas. But there was hope for me
and the city if the Mayor would just accept my proposal.

So, before I arranged my meeting with the Mayor I wrote
out my proposal, which I still have. The proposal was for the
The city of Gary to fund my schooling and in return for the
investment I would return to the city and fix it up step by step.

Dream big or go home, right?

So I went in and talked to the Mayor about the city, giving her the ideas of a man that was now living at his mother's and nothing to call his own. That was reality. No matter how good the ideas were or how much sense they made, I had no power to back me. But, I went in and boldly proposed anyway. She listened, thanked me for coming in and invited me to come to a town hall where she would be announcing to residents that the Obama administration had tapped Gary to be 1 of 7 cities that would receive funding from the HUD department for what was called the Strong Cities, Strong Communities Program.

While there I listened and then went to the microphone because they also let the residents speak. I expressed a little bit clearer the sentiments of the people that had spoken before me and to let the residents know that the Mayor was doing her best. The video is somewhere out there. I also left my proposal with Mr. Antonio Riley who was the HUD regional administrator at that time.

As you may have already concluded she wasn't able to accept my offer with all of the work she had in front of her including the Northside Redevelopment Project which was and still is one of her main focus for a city that was on the decline in every way imaginable. I was very appreciative of the opportunity, but it was time to go. I bid my mom and family farewell once again and off to San Diego I went with a few dollars in my pocket and a dream.

First... The Obstacle

I arrived in San Diego on a greyhound to an Aunt that hadn't seen and spent time with me since I was 3 years old. I was reserved, but Aunt Theresa was not as she bolted towards me with the biggest smile ever and gave me an even bigger hug. It felt so good!

My aunt is a small woman, really compassionate, loving and has her name next to religious in the dictionary. She's much more open now five years later from the first time I met her. We drove to my new place of residence as she inquired about what I have been going through on which I had very little to say. She then started telling me about my uncle, her husband, and my cousins, her two sons, one of which was in high school and the other was of course Marcus. As you can see, my aunt was also someone who liked to talk.

I went into the house and met my uncle LaRunce and cousin LaRunce Jr. whom I had met years ago for the first time when he and my sister Skylah had a dance-off. It was epic for both of them, but his younger cousin

won. He was also a good student, was good at plenty of sports,

and also played guitar.

Uncle 'Runce, on the other hand, was a genius, he built cars

from the ground up, worked as a master electrician at San

Diego State is a master gamer and hates Batman. That's a

battle between him and Marcus. I'm staying out of it. After

meeting them I showered up and went to bed.

I saw my cousin Marcus later in the week for the first time

because he worked, doing what, I forget and lived in an

apartment in downtown. We spent some time together. He's

a cool, tough guy, looks like a pretty boy, health enthusiast, well

known, with a podcast called "(The J.I.G. is Up) a podcast

that focus on Metis Culture."

I spent close to six months there with most of the time being

spent on going to the library and continuing my researching

which now included information about many different types

of religions and acting, specifically the types of acting styles.

I also spent time at a park nearby with a lake and a walking

path where I would sit and write about my hopes to share

Truth with millions of people. This is something I

knew nothing about, but something I felt deep inside of me

for some reason. The way that I would do that would be

through mass media, preferably as an actor. I guess it meant

sharing my truth and it looks like I'm doing it through this book. It's funny how life does what it wants to do.

62 | BALANCING DARK WITH LIGHT

While there in San Diego I had also become a member of
BAPAC which is a non-profit organization that works to
ensure the Black community in San Diego County remains
an economic, social, and political force in Southern
California. This was a great opportunity to meet and learn
from some successful individuals, but I wasn't ready to
jump all the way in. I had to go to L.A. to be an actor. Man,
I was so short-sighted. Or was I?

After overstaying my welcome and not getting a job until
the last month of my stay there, it was time to hit the road again,
but this time I was heading to the city of dreams.

I had already gone and auditioned at the New York Film
Academy and was only able to come up with 2/3 of the
tuition so the point is that I came to the city of dreams
with just that, a dream!

My aunt told me that I was more than likely going to be living
in the homeless shelter which is something that I had never
considered until I was getting on the greyhound to come here.
I had big plans, but how was I going to achieve them?
I arrived in L.A., got off the bus and rolled my suitcase out
to the sidewalk. I breathed in the smog-filled air and thought
to myself, "This is the place where I was going to make it big!"

But first, let me check my phone to find out which homeless the shelter I would be staying at tonight because I didn't want to be staying outside next to this guy that was a few hits away from overdosing. This was my new reality, but it hadn't set in yet.

After searching for places to stay, I found a place called The Union Rescue Mission which was located in an area that I wasn't familiar with named Skid Row. This is known as one

of the scariest places in the world by people all over the country. It was probably worse before, but what I saw couldn't have been too far behind.

I saw, what I came to find out were heroin addicts nodding in and out in one place, bouncing up and down for the 10 minutes that I initially saw them until I finally passed them. There were men in dresses, which wasn't the issue, the the issue is that I'm sure they were on some kind of substance because it looked like they had been wearing their outfit for the last month and they dared to try and flirt with anybody! I may be homeless, but damn it I have class!

There were people selling everything from "allegedly" stolen electronic devices, to single cigarettes, to the tiny alcohol bottles, clothes, whatever drug you needed, and if you liked prostitutes of many different flavors. It was a one-stop shop for everything you don't need.

I think it's safe to say that now the reality was truly starting to kick in. I continued to walk by as if not bother. I had seen some things in my life, so there was no way I could let them see me sweat. This was a reflection of things I had in my mind, but I continued to feel like woe is me and why is the world such a grim, dark place. I doubt that I had ever been lower than this.

And then I walked inside. The people that checked me in was as professional as they could be, considering that they had to kick somebody out, who was more than likely on a completely different planet at the time. Something that they probably have to deal with every hour on the hour.

64 | BALANCING DARK WITH LIGHT

They had a storage room down the hall from the showers where we all kept our luggage with our clothing inside so I took my bag there and went to what people call the TV room that had one small TV where we all watched whatever was on. Here and the resting place right next to, but outside of the room is where I spent my first week in what I now know was a state of shock.

The upstairs was even more shocking. It's an open area where all the men sleep on bunk-beds. There were hundreds of beds, all full of men congregating, laughing, arguing, fighting, farting, stealing and whatever else that was going on when I was asleep.

Yes, I had no problem going to sleep. This is where not showing any feelings came in handy. I'm pretty sure I looked just as crazy as anyone, well almost anyone in the room. All I did was read my books and talk as little as possible.

There were many entertaining conversations, some of the people that had seen what we think of as glory and others that made no sense whatsoever. This was the world I was living in. During my time there I continued to go to the library to get far away from Skid Row and to continue looking for the meaning of life.

I was part of the Missions Gateway Program which was and still is a 30-day program. I may talk about the conditions as if I wasn't grateful and at that time I wasn't. I saw everything around me negatively even when I was getting the help I so desperately needed.

First... The Obstacle | 65

Well, my 30 days came and went faster than I could make enough money to find a place to stay, with the help of the staff members I transferred across the street to another homeless shelter named The Weingart Center which is another Non-Profit Organization.

This particular place has a 90-day open door program that

has counselors and services that helps link clients to mental, physical, substance abuse, and workforce development programs. They also require you to save 75% of your income. Here they were stricter and I had a counselor check on me once or twice a week. I also had found a job while searching online working for Dialogue Direct, a for-profit organization that promotes and fundraises for different non-profit organization.

The particular charity that I was fundraising for was called Children International, a children's charity that asks people to sponsor children all over the world. So when I read about it online I was sold.

My actual job was to go out to all of the greater Los Angeles areas, stop people from doing whatever it was that they were doing and persuade them to hand over their credit card to someone that they had just met to sponsor a child in Zambia, Africa. Just imagine if they had known I lived in a homeless shelter on Skid Row! I did my job and I did it well.

I did it so well that I consistently found myself on our office leader's board. This was an office that had some of the most confident people in all of L.A. and they were not afraid to

show it. These were some of the biggest egos I had ever been around.

Some of them were recording artists that had an actual record deal, others were pretty well known DJ's, people that could talk women to do whatever they wanted, in this case it was to just sponsor a child from poverty, but who knows what else was happening, and another who has a show on TLC right now. The fact is I was putting up numbers in line with extremely motivated people, go-getters and it felt amazing. I guess reading all those self-help books were beginning to show some promise after I put in some action. I was finally making and saving money. I was feeling good about myself so I took some of my money and started acting class at Playhouse West in North Hollywood. It was awesome. This school used the Meisner technique which is a technique to get out of one's head which is what I needed to do.

I had also gone for a run one morning, which was something that I rarely did and had come across a man passing out flyers for a meditation that guided people how to reflect and release negative patterns that had been created in their mind that would then allow the person to be fully in the moment. It all sounded interesting and went along with everything that I had been reading and was coming to understand so I went to their introduction to hear more. I liked what I heard so I began this releasing meditation that same evening. Looks like it was time for a new journey which usually entails new obstacles to overcome.

Meditation?

It was a brand new day, but I still lived a homeless shelter
and I would have all types of emotional outbursts when things
don't go my way while canvassing at work. I was a good guy

and I always stayed positive so it must've been the fault of the people that I was meeting though, right? Maybe it was or maybe it wasn't, I sure as hell didn't know at the time. All I knew was that something still felt off and I had hoped that meditating could help.

When I had gone to the introductory seminar I listened intently as they explained in simple terms that a humans pain and sorrows stemmed from the fact that we all had been born with, and had taken the information of everything since birth, into our minds and had created a world that we and we alone had been living in and how this has disconnected us from our source, whatever we may call it. It made sense to me.

68 | BALANCING DARK WITH LIGHT

They then explained how we could reflect on our life and release those fundamental roots that we had consciously and subconsciously been storing within ourselves. All we had to do was close our eyes and follow let it go, and that we could go at a pace that was comfortable for us. It was right in line with what I had been reading and taking in so even though some people decided not to start and to do more research, I began immediately.

My first session would be the next day after I finished work, acting class, and before I went back "home." I was excited about going to the center because I had a good, but stressful day stopping people on the street, and I also had a good day in class. I went in and they once again explained what the goal of what I was doing. Which was to release what was making me react in ways that I didn't like. But the first couple of days I was just going to be reflecting over my entire life as much as I could to have some type of order when I began letting go.

It was very interesting, also very scary and intimidating to reflect on the life that I had lived, so for me; it was challenging to do so. As I tried to reflect, my mind was blank, but I could remember some things that happened and those little things I could remember brought emotions right along with them which was very uncomfortable. As I explained this to them they assured me that it was natural and that we would be letting them go at the next session which then motivated me to come back.

When I came back the next time we began using the method to let go and release the emotions. It wasn't easy because I thought it was just bullshit at the beginning, but I stayed and

kept trying because what else did I have to do? To my surprise by the end of the session when all was said and done I felt lighter than I did than when I had first arrived. I went home as I had just smoked some really good weed, more stable. I was impressed.

I continued to meditate and go to class for the next couple of months. I was making a name for myself at Playhouse West, both for the times when my talent would shine through and when my past would shine through which was extremely embarrassing.

Because the acting class was one where we had to let whatever emotions come out and the meditation class was to release emotions as well, they went hand and hand together; on most days. On other days it was a different story. I would be on stage in the middle of a scene that required some form of happiness, but instead what would come out is some form of some deep, weird sadness. This was not a good look, period! So now I had a decision to make. Do I stop meditating which was helping me, but also seemed to be hurting me or do I stop the acting class that would possibly help me get to the goal that I had for myself before I came to L.A.? The meaning of life or acting. It would be nice to have both, but the meaning of life won out in this instance.

Honestly, at that moment it wasn't that deep! It was more like having the fear of what my classmates would think about me if I continued to make a donkey of myself on stage and or going to close my eyes and leave this crazy world behind for a while.

But, it was okay because maybe a month or two later I picked up stand-up comedy. This too is something that I enjoyed. The thought to begin doing it came from wanting to express myself and be heard, but I didn't consider what stand-up really meant. I just thought I had to get up on stage, act silly, and tell cool jokes. Nope! There was also this thing called timing and mine were more than a tad bit off.

Now I performed about three times and all of them were pretty much the same. I would go in so scared you could smell it on me, but I looked cool as a cucumber, so I didn't think anyone would notice. I would get up on stage, get in front of the mic and just started talking like I thought a comedian was supposed to talk, yeah I got a couple laughs, but what's weird is that when I did, I would get more nervous and start forgetting the words that I wrote for a three-minute set. Who does that? Me, that's who. I promise it felt more like six and a half minutes instead. That was fun.

This was a recurring pattern that I had picked up; I would be doing well, nobody would be responding and I would wonder why they hate me, and then people would respond to me positively and I would wonder if they liked me.

Welcome to my world. This is why I stopped doing stand-up too and focused on saving children and meditation from here on.

As I continued to meditate I felt as though I was on a

psychological and emotional roller coaster and it showed

more at work than it did anywhere else because I

had to be open. I was able to see that I had some deep anger

and unfortunately it would come out on some of the potential

sponsors. Especially after someone had just walked by and

told me to get a real job or told me to get the fuck out of their

way. I would hold on to all that and it would just explode out

onto someone else that would have a genuine question that I

would take personally. It was bad.

I had saved up enough money thanks to the program I was

in and I was getting pretty upset with myself for my behavior

at work so to alleviate some of the stress I asked the

meditation instructors if I could move in to get away from Skid

Row.

After I moved in I began meditating more frequently to

overcome all of the thoughts, feelings, and emotions that I

was having. These were very painful to go through, but the

best part about it was that I could stay locked away and not

be bothered by anyone. I could go for walks if I needed to and

just get up and go to work the next day as if nothing ever

happened. The small things.

It was right up my alley. I could have crazy thoughts and

yet hide them away from others, but the only difference was

that I couldn't hide them away from myself any longer and that scared me and empowered me.

I continued to do well at work, getting many children sponsored and moving up the ladder while gaining respect. There were questions from my co-workers about how I was able to maintain, especially since I was living in a shelter. They also questioned me deciding to move into a meditation center, but I paid it no mind. I didn't even know these questions were going on behind my back. Nonetheless, I put in my two weeks-notice to focus even more on releasing and overcoming my past. At that time I had found out from someone about what was going on in the office.

72 | BALANCING DARK WITH LIGHT

After my two weeks passed I started meditating 10hrs at a time. As one could imagine there were many realizations about myself that I would have never admitted to had I not continuously reflected on my life and seen the perspective that I had. I realized that I had to accept responsibility and be accountable to not just some of the things in my life, but everything in my life. That includes all the moments and events that happened when I was a child. Crazy, right?

Yes, I thought so too because even though I came to that realization once or twice I still made sure in my real, everyday life to blame at least 10 people per day and you, a person that's reading this book, might have been one of them.

I was more than 6 months in and as you can tell I was making progress, but I still had a lot of work to do when it came to overcoming myself and the crazy world that I had built for myself. Something else you may be questioning is if this meditation was helping or making matters worse and I would say yes to both of those questions. Sometimes I finished a session more stressed than I was before and on those days I was ready to quit.

There were many times when I had to take a day or maybe even a week off, but sometimes I needed that time to make sure I was doing the right thing and I wasn't being brainwashed and other times I took days off because I felt like I had overcome all the stresses of life. There was never a dull moment. Just like I liked!

Meditation? | 73

When I had started these meditation instructors told me that this journey wouldn't be easy. But, damn! They didn't say I would have to go a full 12 rounds with Mike Tyson in his prime though! At least that's what it felt like sometimes. I also never would have thought that "I" was a more worthy opponent than Mike Tyson in his prime. I was flabbergasted.

Because I realized that I had much more work to do I talked to the instructors about going to a retreat center that they had in South Korea. I asked them about pricing and what all I would need to attend. All I would need is a passport which at that time I knew nothing about and I was already 27 years of age.

When I found out the price of everything, I then had to come up with a plan to make money so I decided to go back to what I knew best. Saving children from poverty! I had a goal to go save as many children as possible and save $5,000. I went to work almost every day motivated to talk to people and let them know the problem, which was that in underdeveloped countries some children have a much harder time getting the essentials that we as Americans take for granted and that by taking a small amount of their time and resources they can help change at least one child's life for the better. Who knows what will happen next, whether this child would do this or do that, but what we know is that he or she will have a chance to make a choice. And that was something to be proud of.

See I told you I was good at my job. Anyway, this is an approach that I took to get people involved for the next three months and get involved they did! Helping me to achieve my goal putting me on the track to Korea.

The instructors were surprised at how fast I came up with the money. I went out, got my passport during the time that I was working, got my plane ticket three weeks before my flight with Korean Air, which is pretty damn awesome, and began my journey heading to Nonson, South Korea

Korean Pilgrimage

Before I left L.A. I was informed of a form of releasing with this meditation was called action meditation. Action meditation was needed because people had to live and socialize and make money and all the other things that come along with being human. So with that fact being known this form of meditation was created to make habits arise within one's body to be released.

It was one thing to sit and come to some understanding with the mind, but could those understandings translate when you were faced with an actual situation staring you right in the face. Having an ideal and living that ideal are two different worlds and I was only living in the ideal world

in my mind making me incomplete from the real world.
I didn't know that so it sounded kind of weird to me, but
somehow still made sense.

76 | BALANCING DARK WITH LIGHT

Anyway I traveled on this amazing airplane with beautiful,
professional individuals that served me well. The food was
delicious and the best part about it is that there was no
upcharge for asking for seconds. So I asked for thirds on this
16hr trip from West to East, before landing on a beautiful
Friday evening to Incheon Airport where I took more than
enough photos.

I was also the only Black person there, making me feel both
special and self- conscious. I think this made it very easy
for my driver to spot me. I was the only "unique" person at
this airport.

An older Korean about 50-60 who spoke little English,
picked me up and welcomed me to Korea. He told me to
enjoy this night because we would be taking a 3-hour drive
the next morning to what he called headquarters.

We arrived at the Incheon local center and to my surprise,
they had pizza and spaghetti, two things that the figured
would make me feel American. They were right. I felt right
at home. One because it was a habit to be able to find comfort
anywhere where I could close my eyes and rest through the

night and two, it was interesting and calming to me to see how hard they were working to speak to me in English. Also, jet lag. With all these factors I slept very well that night.

For the record, I hadn't overcome all of my internal issues so yes, I did judge them, a lot, even though they did their best to accommodate me. I was so small-minded that I judged everything from their look, the way they talked, and the way they walked. I was impressed when I saw that one of

the instructors dressed in a way that I thought was cool. He even walked coolly. I was genuinely shocked! Don't judge me.

I woke up the next morning and they had an amazing American breakfast; Sausage, eggs, and toast, with coffee. I had the biggest smile on my face and some gratefulness in my heart. I was thankful that I had something good to eat not because they had put in energy and effort to make me feel comfortable. Good thing I was here to do more meditation. After we finished eating, we gathered everything, headed to the SUV loaded up and started the next phase of my trip. I know I said this man barely spoke English, but somehow we ended up having a three-hour-long conversation and most of the talking was done by him. Especially since I still had a hard time opening up to people. It would get pretty awkward real quick if it were up to me at that time.

If it were up to me, I would probably start with asking him about how long he had been meditating, which would be a good start, and then as it got too silent, ask him about his family, which might have been too much, and then get real defensive and weird when he asked about mine. Okay, my point is that it was better that he took over the conversation because he spoke better English than I did Korean. He mostly spoke of and taught me a lot about Korea and some of its history. I guess it was good that I had brought a book about Korea that I had checked out of the library so I could join in on a little of the conversation.

We talked about the Korean-Japan war where Japan annexed Korea and harshly ruled over the country for over 30

years. He wasn't too happy about that as he told me that there was still tension between the countries, especially the elders. He let me know that there was always some resistance to the oppression sometimes in public, but mostly behind the scenes. The end of World War II is what liberated them from Japan and three years later they were up and running their own government.

I also asked him about the Korean War that started a few years later where America backed the South and The Soviet backed the North. He mostly spoke about how families were broken away from each other and had spent decades not knowing what had happened to each other.

He talked to me about the fact that South Korea was one of the poorest countries in the world for about 15 years after breaking away from Japan and then again from the North. He told me that they were mostly an agricultural economy, but started rapid growth from the 60s to the 90s where it became a prosperous industrial country and is now one of the deserving countries of great respect around the world.

He asked me if I knew how to play ping pong or was familiar with taekwondo because he was good at ping pong and me unfortunately had never played and he was proud that taekwondo had been a sport that began in Korea many years before.

I told him I played baseball for many years and how much I loved it and that I was pretty good at it. He told me he would show me how to play ping pong. It was a great

experience and it made me respect the Korean culture much more.

I also liked that they show great appreciation to teachers and pay them well.

Well, here we are now. We had arrived and it was a Saturday. A day when all the local centers in Korea visited so when I arrived it had a festive feeling in the atmosphere.

I had come a long way, both literally and figuratively. This had to be my life's path considering the sequence of events from my childhood to the times that I had lost everything, making me question the meaning of life. From there beginning a quest for Truth, starting with reading many books on the subject from The Practical Neuroscience of Buddha's Brain, to Dark Night of the Soul, Conversations With God, The Power of Now, and a lesser-known heavyweight, The Way to Become a Person in Heaven While Living. Long title, but a great book. It was written by the founder of this meditation that guides people on how to use the big mind to release the little mind. This was a person who just wanted to meditate in the mountains near his home after retiring from owning a prep school. He ended up discovering absolute truth and was now on a mission to share how anyone can do just that.

If it were me I would've just relaxed while letting a younger person run my school while sitting back and enjoying the fruits of my labor. In 1996 he began teaching others how to achieve the same thing in and hasn't stopped ever since. Now there are over 300 centers worldwide, all of them independently owned and

operated. While these centers are being run he travels from country to country giving seminars and teaching people the method to become their true selves.

I've observed, complained, and judged the whole time I had been meditating, skeptical and ready to run away every step of the way. I continuously checked my mind to make sure nothing weird was being done to my thought process. But all I could see was that I was more sharp, understanding, more compassionate, and accepting of myself most importantly, and to others as well. So because that's what I experienced I had no problem coming to this big beautiful center in the middle of this big, beautiful mountain.

I was happy but also scared shitless because at this point I still had a long way to go, but here I was putting in the work to hopefully find my true self thanks to this simple method and the person who created it. I even made sure to let go of the concept of this being the only way and this person being the only one.

This main center had two main buildings; in one there was the main office, sleeping quarters for the lower level meditators, the showers, and a lounge area where I met a couple of women from America. One of the women had the same name as a Japanese woman that I had been dating. Yeah, maybe I shouldn't have brought that up because... awkward!

Behind this building was an area where people could smoke, socialize, and let all the amazing trees help alleviate all of the worries and fears that had been getting released during the class.

The other main building was where the cafeteria was connected with the secondary office, and the classroom for the higher level meditators. Behind this building was a smaller area where the kitchen staff and students all rested and relaxed during their breaks.

Next to that building was a convenient store that sold all kinds of Korean goodies including red bean ice cream which Koreans go crazy for, but I'm not a big fan.

Connected to it was a restaurant that sold everything from sausage and eggs made by an American who had been living there and your favorite Korean dishes. I came to realize that I was a fan of their spicy rice cakes. This is where people came who wanted something other than what was on the menu.

Next to that was the barbershop and a gigantic open field where people played soccer and socialized. It was also a place for the children to run around when they had a break from the children's center close by.

The day-care service is where the children were cared for but the center also took care of the families that lived there and ran the day to day business.

Speaking of business I had decided before I had

left L.A. that I would focus on letting go as much as possible, partly because I wanted to get rid of all my stress and partly because I didn't want anybody bothering me. And then it was time for dinner. I guess I had no choice but to be bothered! The good news is that I was feeling great after arriving there and being surrounded by so much positive energy so I had a really good time meeting people. We sang songs together. Songs by well-known artists from

82 | BALANCING DARK WITH LIGHT

all over the world. And the food was just as good. Well maybe except for the kimchi. Although I have come to at least be able to tolerate it nowadays. I love the kimchi fried rice! I found out that whenever newcomers would visit the center they would go and explore the mountains on Sundays, so since the next day was Sunday we all made plans to go hiking and see what it was about.

The next day came and off to the mountains we went, running into multiple vendors at the foot of them that were selling everything from snacks, food, accessories, and clothes. It was completely unexpected but very welcomed.

As we were climbing up we came across a few Buddhist temples where they invited us inside to show us the deep, rich history of how and when they were built. The architectural structures were amazing. As we continued up there was a small stream where some of us took off our shoes and got our feet massaged by the fish swimming by.. The overall experience was so serene, fun, and peaceful.

We left the mountains and headed back to the center to prepare for lunch. My mindset was to go back, eat and head straight back to my room and get some rest. But first, food! It was another amazing set of events that included meeting some of the older students and having the younger students ask me questions like, how was L.A., have I met any movie stars, and if they could touch my hair. Yes, as if I was a dog. I understood, though, so I decided to let them. I also kind of wanted to punch the guy that had asked.

As soon as I finished my meal I left out and came across some more people from all over the world like Sweden, Australia, Japan, Iceland, and even Kenya! I was shocked! We talked as much as possible because people were staying at different times. Some were staying for one week, two weeks, and I was staying for three months. Yes, I was making sure I got as much work as possible!
After being pleasantly surprised that there were more people than just me and the few members in L.A. that I had met I left and went to my room to meditate until I fell asleep. I was awoken three hours later by my roommate to get

ready for dinner. I waited and meditated in my room and reflected on the time I had been there until the end of dinner because I had a rush of emotions arise while I was reflecting before I had fallen asleep and when I woke up there was strong anger in my mind and I didn't know where it had come from. I also wasn't comfortable enough with myself to be around people when I didn't feel like it. My main focus was to make it until tomorrow without setting any friendly fires. My next month was spent just like a monk pretty much with a fair share of human contact now and again. For the record, there were people there of all types, including those that skipped classes and found significant others and more than likely left the premises to take there dates to the next level. I just chose to be the way that I was because of my personality and my mindset.

84 | BALANCING DARK WITH LIGHT

After that month of hiding my problems from people, it was time for action meditation. Now it was time to see if I would physically fight someone.

My first duty was to clean and mop the building where the main office was. This was probably so they could keep an eye on the creepy quiet guy that kept to himself and that's where all the new people had usually started. At least that's what I thought. It was me and another person so the only person I could blame whenever I had a problem myself. I had never realized how active my mind was until I was alone consciously checking to see what was going on.

Before I had even begun this practice I would find myself always surrounded by people, keeping me from having any access to my thoughts in general and my thought patterns specifically, but now I found myself more sensitive to every little thing. It was super annoying because I couldn't deny it anymore.

I also felt more vulnerable, another reason why I wanted to stay away from people. It was as if I was still smoking weed and was feeling like everybody knew what I was thinking and why I was thinking about what I was thinking. It was both a great ability to have and super frustrating that I was unable to turn it off.

I was also able to notice that I would try to rush through my work because I didn't want to be doing it. Even though I had nothing else to do or no place to go I still habitually rushed and got frustrated, I guess at the broom and mop for not moving fast enough. These habits I would notice, but couldn't fix. What I found out is that my mind could know the "right"

way or "wrong" way to do things, but that didn't mean my body would automatically follow. My body had repetitively done things my whole life and those repetitions wouldn't change unless I continuously battled and overcame it which could take years.

As I was slowly figuring this out on my own with the guidance I received it was time to move on to another form of action. This time it was picking sesame leaves at the sesame farm. This was strenuous on my back and knees because I had to bend over again and again and I was not as nimble as the women that were also getting frustrated, but making it look easier than I was.

So many thoughts flooded my mind exposing the fact that I wasn't as nice and polite as I displayed to other people. I had thoughts like, why the hell do they have me doing this shit, or I wish this lady would stop fucking talking to me. Other thoughts included but were not limited to, it's too damn hot out here or damn my back hurts! I couldn't wait to get back inside where the air conditioner was.

We would do action, have a break, do the action again have lunch, do more action, have another break, have dinner, have a break, and then finish the night with a sitting meditation session to reflect on and let go of all the different types of mind that had come up during the day. The problem with that, at least initially was that I was too damn sleepy to stay awake during night meditation causing me to nod in and out until I just gave up, laid down and fell asleep.

Although I was going through many difficulties, knowing
that I wasn't the only one made it a little bit easier.

86 | BALANCING DARK WITH LIGHT

The sad part is that whenever we, the students would talk
about it together I would always try and sugarcoat the way I
felt where the others had no problem sharing what
instructor they hated or why they were going to try to change
their work for something easier.

It was all good because as I continued to go out and give my
best effort, I noticed that I was making steady progress with
fewer thoughts flooding my mind due in part to the fact that I
was able to stay awake and let go during night meditation. So
not only was my body getting stronger, but my mind was
feeling lighter.

I felt I was making great progress, but I still had a way to
go and no one else had to point that out for me. It was very
apparent to me and anyone else that paid attention, but by
the time my three months arrived I felt so good that no one
could tear down my pride.

During my time there I had made some good connections with
people and I had managed to piss off and get pissed off by more
than a fair share of people. I hadn't become a master of acceptance,
going with the flow, and disagreeing without being disagreeable.
But I was in a better place than i was before and it showed.It was

almost time to head back to Los Angeles with this new
sense of pride. I also had little gratefulness from following a
method that I didn't create that was helping me overcome my
heartaches and pains. I now know that I wasn't grateful
enough. I pretty much gave all the glory to myself. I guess I
would find out just how great I was on my next journey which
would include helping the L.A. Koreatown center because

that's what I chose to do after seeing the progress that I had
made.

Back to Reality

The flight back home was great! I felt good, I looked good,
so much so that you could smell me throughout the airports.

I was talking to everyone I saw, no matter where they were. Checking in, waiting in line, even outside the airports where people were waiting to be picked up. I was so cool that I brought home a new habit; smoking cigarettes. Something that I had chosen not to do because of my parents. I went to get rid of stress and now I seemed more stressed. At least outside looking in any way.

Everyone that I came across at all the Southern California Centers noticed a difference in me. They weren't short on compliments and of course, I passive-aggressively soaked them all in. Again, I was the super positive guy that was always "okay" with everything. Everything was always "no problem" in my book of denials although I was holding on to a lot of

habits, I still followed a lot of the same ones I had and created a new one that would be easier to eliminate.

So, after a week of taking my victory tour and just laying around putting on the weight that I had just lost. It was time to do some volunteering. It was going to be more action meditation, but this time it would be a little, no, a lot more different. This time I was going to have to face my arch nemesis; humans including the one I hated the most; me. We had a way of reaching out that was very similar to what I was doing as a fund-raiser. A person or people would go out, like the Jehovah's witnesses or people promoting their albums, and reach out to anyone that wanted to listen. Whenever the potential meditator would allow, we would inform them of the fundamentals of the meditation. We would also share the general benefits and the benefits we had personally experienced. If the person was interested, we would invite them to the center for a seminar. We would also inform them of the monthly donation we required for services that would assist in keeping the center open for others and pay the center bills.

After they would sign up for the classes, which are guided, unlimited, usually from 8 am until 10 pm, with full access to all centers worldwide, we would set them up for their first class the next day. From there they would begin the same process that I had gone through, but they would have their world that they had created to go through and overcome at whatever pace that was comfortable with them.

90 | BALANCING DARK WITH LIGHT

There was a lot at stake, but to me, I didn't care to even think that deeply about it. I just ideally wanted to go out and help people from their recurring patterns that kept us doing the same thing and repeating the same lessons over and over again. I was aware of these truths and could talk about them with the best of people, but they hadn't been fully transformed throughout my whole being, and the only way I could find out was by approaching the world and seeing how it responded to me and how I responded to it. So here we go! My first day of promoting was filled with many emotions. I started happy, excited, and motivated, but when I realized I wouldn't be driven to the locations my emotions changed to being discontent and semi-excited.

From that emotional and mental space, I had to walk in the heat bringing out frustration and anger which I tried the walking meditation to overcome, but wasn't yet experienced with yet, so I covered up my feelings with fake happiness and some positive self-talk which helped a little, but not enough. It wasn't enough because when I finally got to my location and started interacting with people, the fact that I was feeling a little better didn't change what was under the surface which is really what God or the Universe responds to. For that very reason the first few people that I came in contact with had no problem telling me that they weren't interested in the most direct, frustrating way possible which in turn brought all of my frustrations to the surface causing me to pray that these feelings would be taken away.

On this, my first day it helped because of the feelings subsided and the next few people, even if they declined my invitation, they did so with kindness that then made me feel better. This was good for me at a time when I was still looking for affirmation from other people.

From there I was able to meet and talk to genuinely interested people. A few of them made reservations and others took flyers and continued about their day. It was an up and down sequence of events all throughout the day and by the time five o'clock came around I was very ready to go back to the center and let go of the whole day.

As I was walking home, I was just reflecting on my time out usually focused on the moments I should have said something differently or the times when someone said something "wrong" to me. I was wondering what I could've done differently to make better outcomes which were good, but I wasn't letting anything go. I also wasn't giving myself any credit for anything at all.

When I arrived at the center, I talked to the main helper about how my day was, of course, denying my true feelings and telling him that it was good and that I had learned a lot, which was technically true, but was emotionally in denial. Completely out of balance.

After speaking with him I went and meditated for about two hours, realizing some of the questions that I had about what I could've done differently. I still wasn't reflecting on my emotions or lack thereof, so I wasn't getting any answers about those, probably because I was blind to the fact that it was an issue.

92 | BALANCING DARK WITH LIGHT

The instructors or helpers had traveled to different countries promoting wherever the founder was doing seminars and with that practice, they came and did the same thing at their own respective centers, focusing solely on Koreans due to the the language barrier and being intimidated by speaking with Americans, mostly due to cultural differences and habits. They still had some things to overcome, but they had surely put in work for years to try and overcome themselves. I would be the first American in L.A. and first African American in the United States to take the steps towards becoming a helper. But, before I or anyone else could become an instructor we had to eliminate some habits like, not running away the potential meditators with anxiety talk, or fear that they might want to harm us because we were suspicious of any humans because of what we had seen our minds.

I started out promoting our Santa Monica center where I would meditate in the morning and then go out for the rest of the day until around 6pm and then come back and meditate before calling it a night. It was interesting to me at least the idea of going out and sharing something that I knew worked and I thought was awesome. I didn't foresee the fact that they didn't see what I saw and didn't know what I knew just like I couldn't see what they saw and couldn't know what they knew. For this reason, I felt as though I wasn't doing well overall because we were all on different pages and I wasn't skilled enough to bridge the gap.

I continued doing the action meditation for the next two and a half years. Most of the time was spent in Santa Monica

where we had grown to have the second most students of the United States centers. I had helped to assist on hundreds of students most who had come and gone within their first month. I realized and enlightened a great deal to what was holding my true self back.

I realized that I was incapable of giving all credit to the The universe truly and practically. I could do it ideally, but not actually, and that was realized in how I would respond in real-time to people I came across where I was extremely inconsistent.

At the time I would make excuses for myself and go about my business without putting much effort into letting go. Little did I know that the changes were happening behind the scenes as much as I was doing which was the exact opposite

of what my body wanted to do, go out and promote
every day with little to no results.

I still went out anyway because although it was a challenge,
I knew that I was continuously changing for the better and I
couldn't keep that to myself. It was the battle of doing what's
best for me or doing what was best for others without seeing
how to balance it out where everyone would benefit from my
actions. I wasn't there yet, but I was making progress in that
enlightened direction.

Because I was making such good results and improving
I was asked to travel to all of our centers in the
Los Angeles area to promote. Doing so allowed me to
encounter even more personalities and see even deeper
within myself.

94 | BALANCING DARK WITH LIGHT

I began to understand that the reason it was such a
challenge was because a lot of the habits that I had were
generationally imprinted in my DNA. I realized this because
I had been actively putting effort into overcoming a lot of
these habits and even when I would see myself doing certain
things at the moment there was still nothing that I could do
to stop them.

I know how that sounds, but it was like the Universe was just
showing me that I, this body that expires after 80 to 100yrs

didn't have the control that I believed I had. All I could

do was laugh at the whole situation and just go through it and

then repent, reflect, and let it go again from my mind until

my body followed later on.

After helping other centers, the time has come for me to

begin training to run a center myself. The issue was that the

other instructors were so busy that they weren't able to

properly train me, so I had to run it to the best of my limited

ability and get help whenever it came which wasn't very

often.

As I mentioned before running a center wasn't my strong

suit. The closest I came to that was standing on a street having

a philosophical conversation with a Christian or some other

spiritual or scientific person. That was good for me from an

egoistic point of view, but for guiding someone towards the

Way it wasn't very conducive.

I had to help them in a way that each person

could understand no matter their background. It was a skill

built for someone who had already overcome themselves or

at least have made it further than what I was capable of

conveying and having no experience with business.

It was a great honor, but one that had its fair share

of fuck ups. The good news is that being aware of the

shortcomings that were within me is exactly the reason that I was a part of this meditation. In that way, the instructor was the instructor and the student, and the student was the student and the instructor, but the only difference was that one was the "instructor" and the other was the "student."

I had come to realize that I still had trouble with expressing myself in the clearest, concise way possible and because of that I confused the students more than I should have. I did well when it came to being friendly and talking about what "I" knew, but the main reason that they were there was to find out themselves.

The sad part about it is that they expected me to teach them something and I did everything I could. This was a problem because it was my position to guide them and it was the Universe's job to teach them.

I had no sense of independence and therefore I latched on to any and everyone to find some form of validation.

This stemmed from a lack of true confidence and wanting to feel wanted and loved. With all the meditation I had done and the many times my mind came to understand these truths I still couldn't do it at the moment.

I was extremely frustrated when I would see how many students would begin, make progress for months and never show up again. What now!? I had done so much and was still failing these people! I lashed out time and time again on the other instructors and even got testy with some of the students.

I had some deep, deep soul searching to do that would get rid of these issues for once and for all because at this point, I felt like I had done all that I could do.

So, from there I did as much action meditation and as much as I could to build the center up. Out of the blue information came that I would need to go out and find a job. Because I was distraught and wasn't making the results that I would've liked that I gave off the impression to others that I wasn't as interested as I was before is what I was informed of.

I was shocked! I was angry and extremely displeased, and I had shared those thoughts and emotions better than I had ever done before. At that moment I knew I had changed and changed a lot. It seemed like I was a completely different person and that scared me because now I had to go out and face the world like I hadn't done before in over five years.! What would happen? How would I be perceived? Did I make as much progress as it seemed? All questions I would've never even conceived of before. Minds had been made up and big change was in the air.

To be in the World and not of It

The change came quick and unexpected and so did the job.
After hearing the news and then expressing myself about how
I felt about the move it was time to move on. After speaking
how true I felt it made it much easier to accept.
Which is probably the reason why I had a job within four
days.
A person that I had been meditating with for a while worked
at a restaurant in Beverly Hills where he had been well
respected by the general manager and he had put in a good
the word for me making it much easier for the new transition that
I was having in my life. A transition that I would've never
made if it were up to "me".

If it were my decision I would've stayed at the center and helped out as much as possible, but it seemed as though I had outgrown that part of the spiritual contract in my life and that it was time to do what I was here to do. But first I had to clean up any and everything that would prevent me from doing my life's purpose.

So, I started at this position as a cashier, being shown again that true confidence and humility would be the only way to move forward to something that I still needed to tweak, obviously. This was something that my managers, co-workers and the people on public transportation would be giving me a quick, hard lesson on.

I started out working five days a week meaning I would have to be on a bus at least ten times a week. I felt as though this was a problem because I was so sensitive and so in tune and vulnerable, so whenever I would have to ride it I would plug my ears with headphones just to find some sense of where I ended and others began.

I then had to go into work where, because the energy that I carried was so intense that would change the whole dynamics and mood of the entire restaurant that it made everyone around me extremely uncomfortable, including myself.

I noticed this phenomenon before, but on a much smaller

scale because I didn't have to be around the same individuals
for five hours at a time. The energy that I have is one that can
be felt from very far away and it seems to make people aware
of information that they have in their psyche that otherwise
would have stayed dormant.

To be in the World and not of It | 99
This happens around anyone that comes in contact with me
and this is something that I was extremely afraid of and
deeply self-conscious about. It's also something that I really
wanted to hide and had felt that it was more of a
curse than a gift.
I had no idea how to control it and I found out that it was
nothing I could do to control so I took the anger and
frustration out on my co-workers whenever they got too fed
up with me.
This made me see, change and tweak some deep, deep, deep
 emotional baggage that I still had within me and the reason
is because I was able to find and eliminate any and all blockages
that I had in my mind. Also the method seemed more powerful.
Not only had the method been changed, but a month after
I began working there was a retreat for all of the centers at
our main Florida center where I spent four days going
deeper than I had gone before because of all the work I had
put in up until then.

While there I had changed the way that I saw life

completely. It's like a switch had been turned off and another

one had been turned on. I was a changed person

when I came back even though I looked the same, smelled the

same, and walked the same. What changed was my

perspective.

When I had come back and settled in for a couple of days it

was time to head back to the bus and in to work and test

how much I had changed. I would make sure I didn't plug my

ears with headphones to see how I would respond to the

people on the bus.

I still felt everything and I was aware of the energy

around me. I also found myself getting occasionally caught up

with the feelings of others and my response to them, but I was

able to correct them almost automatically.

Also when I got to work and my managers and co-workers

decided to be my tests I was able to achieve success by seeing

and noticing what happened and continue to focus on what

was needed from me at that moment. I was much more aware.

I was able to have a more comfortable and deeper

connections with them even when we would have intense

challenging conversations. I found myself being able to

express whatever I needed to at any given time which was not possible just one year before.

If I needed to be sad, I was sad, when I needed to be angry, I was angry and any other way I needed to be, I was. I was all these ways, but I wasn't getting caught up in them anymore.

Some of the other ways that I noticed my progression was meeting and conversing with the Beverly Hills residents. The conversations were much more fluent than before and I was able to provide my point of view, no matter what they thought or felt about a situation while being as thoughtful and respectful as possible.

I also had come across a film producer during this time that had just won awards for the best picture. The picture is named Green Book. I hadn't thought too much about doing any

entertainment work since the very beginning of meditation, but after having a conversation with him I had a deep thought comes to me that wouldn't go away.

My thought was to start back doing something that could utilize my talents, allow me to express my experiences, and help heal others in the process. So from there, I decided that the best way to do that with no platform was to start with stand-up. This way I could see how comfortable I was around people that would for sure judge every little thing I do.

I began writing and during the writing, I had the idea to talk

about some things of my past that had been very hard to talk

about before which was the paranoia of my step-father.

Coming up with the content was easy, but I still had a few

more lessons to learn, like putting in the work long enough to

have it manifest into something of quality and

substance.

Because I didn't quite have a grasp on this truth before

the audition that I went on was one to learn from and not one to

tell that I was ready to take my message to a wider audience.

I took my lesson and gathered more information from

someone who had been in the stand-comedy field for decades

and left not expecting anything to come from my

performance moving forward.

From there I was contemplating if I should move forward

or not. I had completely let it go and kept working at the

Chinese restaurant where I had met another man that after

having a conversation, invited me to a day house party of

his that he was having a month later at his Beverly Hills

mansion. I knew that these

were all pointers telling me to keep going forward because

there was some type of shift happening.

Later that week I received an email from Flapper's comedy

club inviting me back to perform at a Saturday evening show. I was super stoked and grateful for the opportunity to do what I had initially planned to do was heal myself and others.

This time, for three weeks straight I wrote, edited and practiced my routine over and over and over again. As I was preparing myself for the show I invited as many people as I could to make sure that I kept myself accountable. I had to make sure that everyone that would be showing up would be satisfied so that meant that I had to be satisfied and satisfied I was. After I finished the show, I got a really good response from the people and I got a video to share with anyone that would watch.

I was really happy and now it was time to head to this party and see what would happen with this newfound confidence and acceptance of whatever that was coming my way. When I arrived, I noticed that the guy that invited me was pretty well-known person considering the faces a demeanor of the guests that I had met. It was people there that any movie watcher would know in the United States and beyond.

I was much more in tune with myself. So much so that I was well known and accepted by everyone I had come across. Although the energy that I carried still had the same effect I didn't pay it any mind and I made sure that I gave myself every opportunity to shine weather I was accepted or not. All

I did was enjoy myself and I found out that, that's all I had to do.

Meanwhile back at work, I was being tested once again, this time even more because I was up for a promotion within the next two weeks, but between that period I had another show to do that I was preparing for.

The first one was to bring awareness to anxiety and how I was able to overcome it by metaphorically speaking about the releasing of internal pain. This one would be about how I lived my life not paying attention to my actual surroundings in my hometown and how through letting go and giving my problems to my "imaginary" friend, and how I now felt like I was in a whole new world, even though I was physically in the same place.

Leading up to the second show I had some deep habits come up to be overcome dealing with belief in myself. The feelings and thoughts were so intense that I went to Griffith Park to hike the mountains and sit and meditate so I could get grounded. This all happened on the same day as the show and because I dealt with what was in my awareness I was able to get grounded and it showed because I had another great show where people came up to me and credited me with originality and depth which were sincere and because of that

I felt very grateful.

As my understanding and faith in God, the Universe grew,
it seemed I would be tested more and more and this all came
in the form of being challenged at work. It seemed I needed to
pass one more test. That was the test of being codependent

which is something that I had come naturally accustomed to,
but it was time to break free.

I had tried to get help from the movie producer to get my
foot in the acting door to no avail, I also tried to get the guy
Sol who had invited me to introduce me to an agent and that
fell through, and now I had to make a dramatic decision to
keep this job or to break free from it and go all-in with what I
knew my purpose was.

So I did the one thing that 97% of people on the planet
wouldn't do. I quit my job not knowing exactly where it
would lead me to because I had nothing concrete to fall back
on except for the fact that I had been getting "signs" from the
world to make all these unorthodox decisions.

Because I had these synchronistic happenings going on all
around me, I came to the idea to write a book that turned out
to be this personal short story that you are now reading. The
book was finished and turned in and sent out after I had been
denied many times by literary agents that I wanted to

represent me.

I guess what I found out is that I had been going through
life believing that what I knew was the truth, but when I found
a meditation with the radical idea that the only way to find one's
true self was to let go and get rid of what I thought my true self was.
It would then bring me right back to the person I always was without
the excess baggage and hang-ups.

This was an extremely scary and uncomfortable road that I
have been traveling on, but it's one that I would invite anyone

to try. There will never be a dull moment and it will
for sure feel like an emotional rollercoaster, but the end does
justify the means. The only way to find out is to do it yourself.
As we all know, everybody is on their path to get to a place
that we all know exists somewhere on the other side of what
we can see, smell, taste, hear, and touch. We all know that
these paths are all valid and hopefully they're well respected.
I also know that from my personal experience that the
meditation that I practice has been a superhighway to that
same destination.

My purpose for writing this story of my life is to help heal
the world and make it a better place in a way that's open,
inspiring, and sincere. Going through and sharing my ups,
downs, and vulnerabilities. I think this is the way to

make the world a better place.

By reflecting on ourselves and keeping and making ourselves accountable for our own lives because the truth lies in realizing that I am the problem which can also make me the solution if I can become truly selfless by doing the same thing that all true nature does which stands independently while giving myself to others without expecting anything in return that's empowering for me. IT CAN BE DONE. We're connected as siblings on such a deep level so I don't mind the love, criticism, or downright hate because that's what family does. All I can do is come from a place of real, raw love. The kind of love that will make you feel something one way or another. The kind of love that will make you question yourself, your decisions, and strive to become a

better you. In return for you becoming a better you that will, in turn, make the world a much better place. Thank you

Acknowledgment

First of all, I have to thank my Creator. That existence which was, before all that is. Call it whatever you want. I want to thank my Mom and Dad, yes both of them for playing major roles in my life. I want to thank my brothers, sisters, and all family members, blood and extended. I want to thank my ancestors and the angels that have helped me along this path. I also want to thank mankind for being my inspiration for writing this book and doing what I can to help the world.

Thank you!!!

Made in the USA
Monee, ÎL
27 August 2020